Selected Writings of
Alexander Berkman

Classic Essays from One of America's Most Influential Anarchist Theorists

by Alexander Berkman

Introduction by Lenny Flank

Red and Black Publishers, St Petersburg, Florida

Introduction (c) 2014 by Red and Black Publishers

Contents

Introduction   5

The Need Of Translating Ideals Into Life   9

The Confession of a Convict   15

The Only Hope of Ireland   21

Deportation, Its Meaning and Menace: Last Message to the People of America   25

The Russian Revolution and the Communist Party   55

The Kronstadt Rebellion   85

The Russian Tragedy: (A Review and An Outlook)   117

The Tenth Anniversary of the Russian Revolution   141

America and the Soviets   147

The Anarchist Movement Today   151

The Bolshevik Dictatorship At Work   157

The Paris Commune and Kronstadt   165

The Awakening Starvelings   173

The Idea is the Thing   177

The Jobless   185

Some Reminiscences of Kropotkin   189

Introduction

Ovsei Osipovich Berman was born in 1870 in the city of Vilnius, the capital of Lithuania. His father was a well-off Jewish shoemaker. Like all Jews at that time in the Russian Empire, the Berkman family was restricted to living in a ghetto called "The Pale", but in 1877, Osip Berkman's social position was high enough that the Tsar's authorities granted his family permission to move to St Petersburg. While there, his son Ovsei changed his name to the more Russian-sounding "Alexander".

Alexander Berkman was sent to an elite "gymnasium" for a classical education, where he proved to be a brilliant student. But as an idealistic young teenager, Berkman was soon caught up in politics. By 1880, a wave of radicalism had swept across Russia, as resentment grew against the Tsarist regime and the crushing economic poverty in the countryside. On March 1, 1881, a student revolutionary group called the *Narodnaya Volya* ("The People's Will") blew up Tsar Alexander II as his car passed Berkman's school—the explosion shattered the windows of his classroom. Five student members of the *Narodnaya Volya* were arrested and executed. Young Berkman was inspired by their idealism and dedication, and was drawn into the radical student movement. He was particularly influenced by his uncle Mark Natanson. Natanson had already been arrested three times by the Tsarist secret police and had been exiled to Siberia, but escaped, returned to St Petersburg, and helped form the student revolutionary group *Zemya y Volya* ("Land and Freedom"). Natanson would be arrested and sent to Siberia twice more before leaving for Europe.

In 1882, Osip Berkman died, the family shoe business was sold, and the Berkman family was ordered by Tsarist authorities to move to the Jewish ghetto in Kovno. Soon afterwards, Alexander began distributing smuggled radical pamphlets to his fellow students at the new school. In 1885, at age 15, Berkman was expelled from school after submitting an essay entitled "There is No God". In 1887, Berkman's mother died, and in 1888, at the age of 18, he decided to emigrate to the United States. He was already a committed anarchist.

In New York City, Berkman joined several anarchist groups, and worked as a typesetter for the anarchist newspaper *Freiheit*, run by German radical Johann Most, who advocated the use of dynamite in "revolutionary attacks" on police, robber barons, and government officials. In 1889, Berkman met Emma Goldman, a fellow anarchist immigrant from Russia. They moved in together and became inseparable partners for the rest of their lives.

By 1892, Berkman and Goldman had moved to Worcester, Massachusetts, where they made a living by selling lunches to local workers. That year, the Homestead Steel Strike broke out in Pennsylvania against the Carnegie Steel Company. The Steel Company's manager, Henry Frick, hired strikebreakers from the Pinkerton Detective Agency, and gunfights broke out between strikers and strikebreakers. Nine strikers and seven Pinkertons were killed. Berkman, inspired by Most and his idea of "propaganda of the deed", decided to make a dramatic gesture which he hoped would provoke the working class into revolutionary action. Berkman traveled to Pittsburgh, where, on July 23, he burst into Frick's office and shot him twice. Frick survived, and Berkman was sentenced to 22 years in prison.

Berkman's attack on Frick resulted in a massive police crackdown on anarchists, all over the country. It also provoked a political split, between anarchists who supported violent actions and those who did not. One of Berkman's fellow prisoners, who had been a Homestead striker, told Berkman that he was an outsider and his action had accomplished nothing. Even Johann Most, who had advocated "propaganda of the deed" for years, now wrote that it was a "total failure", and did nothing more than bring police repression and popular resentment against the anarchist movement. By the time Berkman got out of jail in 1905, after having served 14 years of his sentence, his views had matured. He was no longer interested in symbolic violence to "inspire" the workers--now he realized that only organization and solidarity could bring about a revolution.

After writing an account of his years in jail (published in 1912 as *Prison Memoirs of an Anarchist*), Berkman became an editor for Emma Goldman's anarchist newspaper *Mother Earth*. Then, in April 1914, striking workers at a Rockefeller-owned coal mine in Ludlow, Colorado, were attacked by a group of Pinkertons, state militia, and hired strikebreakers, who fired on the striker's camp with machine guns and then set it afire. Thirteen strikers were killed. Outraged by the Ludlow Massacre, Berkman joined with a number of local anarchists to organize a mass demonstration outside Rockefeller's house in New York City. At some point, a plan was hatched to bomb the Rockefeller house, which went awry when the bomb exploded prematurely and killed the people who were making it. Berkman's apparent involvement in the plot led to a split with Goldman. Berkman left *Mother Earth*, moved to San Francisco, and founded a new anarchist journal of his own, called *The Blast*.

But when the US entered the First World War in 1917, Berkman and Goldman reconciled and began traveling together making speeches against the war, against the military draft, and against the draconian new Espionage Act, which made it illegal to criticize the US government or to speak out against the war. In 1917, both Berkman and Goldman were arrested. Over the next two years, waves of mass arrests, known as the "Palmer Raids", rounded up over 100,000 Americans—members of the anarchist movement, the IWW, labor unions, the newly-formed Communist Party, and the Socialist Party (including elected Socialists who were serving in Congress and in state legislatures)—and charged them with "sedition". Many of those arrested were jailed, many more were deported. Berkman was sentenced to two years in jail, and upon his release in 1920, was ordered deported. He and Emma Goldman, also ordered deported, were both placed on board the old transport ship *Buford* and sent to Russia.

Russia, of course, had just undergone the 1917 Revolution, and political radicals of all stripes were flocking to the new "Soviet

Union". Berkman and Goldman both arrived together in the USSR full of enthusiasm and anxious to see the new social order being constructed. Within a year, however, both were disillusioned. Instead of a socialist system of political and economic democracy, they found a police state where the government ruled by terror and where Party bureaucrats grew fat by siphoning wealth from the urban and rural workers. Both Berkman and Goldman left the USSR in 1921 and wrote books detailing their experiences in Russia (Berkman's *The Bolshevik Myth* was published in 1925).

Berkman settled first in Berlin and then in Paris. After writing an introduction to anarchist ideology (published in 1929 as *The ABC of Communist Anarchism*), Berkman faced declining health from prostate cancer. On June 28, 1936, unable to bear the pain of his medical condition any longer, he killed himself with a handgun.

The Need Of Translating Ideals Into Life

From: Mother Earth Vol. V, no 9, November 1910.

One year has passed since the death of Francisco Ferrer. His martyrdom has called forth almost universal indignation against the cabal of priest and ruler that doomed a noble man to death. The thinking, progressive elements throughout the world have voiced their protest in no ambiguous manner. Everywhere sympathy has been manifested for Ferrer, the modern victim of the Spanish Inquisition, and deep appreciation expressed for his work and aims. In short, the death of Ferrer has succeeded — as probably no other martyrdom of recent history — in rousing the social conscience of man. It has clarified the eternally unchanging attitude of the church as the enemy of progress; it has convincingly exposed the State as the crafty foe of popular advancement; it has, finally, roused deep interest in the destiny of the child and the necessity of rational education.

It would indeed be a pity if the intellectual and emotional energies thus wakened should exhaust themselves in mere indignation and unprofitable speculation concerning the unimportant details of Ferrer's personality and life. Protest meetings and anniversary commemorations are quite necessary and useful, in proper time and place. They have already accomplished, so far as the world at large is concerned, a great educational work. By means of these the social consciousness has been led to realize the enormity of the crime committed by the Church and State of Spain. But "the world at large" is not easily moved to action; it requires many terrible martyrdoms to disturb its equilibrium of dullness; and even when disturbed, it tends quickly to resume its wonted immobility. It is the thinking, radical elements which are, literally, the movers of the world, the intellectual and emotional disturbers of its stupid equanimity. They must never be suffered to become dormant, for they, too, are in danger of growing absorbed in mere adulation of the martyr and rhetorical admiration of his great work. As Ferrer himself has wisely cautioned us; "Idols are created when men are praised, and this is very bad for the future of the human race. The time devoted to the dead would be better employed in improving the condition of the living, most of whom stand in great need of this."

These words of Francisco Ferrer should be italicized in our minds. The radicals, especially — of whatever creed — have much to atone for in this respect. We have given too much time to the dead, and not enough to the living. We have idealized our martyrs to the extent of neglecting the practical needs of the cause they died for. We have idealized our ideals to the exclusion of their application in actual life. The cause of it was an immature appreciation of our ideals. They were too sacred for everyday use. The result is evident, and rather discouraging. After a quarter of a century — and more — of radical propaganda, we can point to no very particular achievement. Some progress, no doubt, has been made; but by no means commensurate with the really tremendous efforts exerted. This comparative failure, in its turn, produces a further disillusioning effect: old-time radicals drop from the ranks, disheartened; the most active workers become indifferent, discouraged with lack of results.

It is this the history of every world-revolutionizing idea of our times. But especially is it true of the Anarchist movement. Necessarily so, since by its very nature it is not a movement that can conquer immediate tangible results, such as a political movement, for instance, can accomplish. It may be said that the difference between even the most advanced political movement, such as Socialism, and Anarchism is this: the one seeks the transformation of political and economic conditions, while the goal of the other includes a complete transvaluation of individual and social conceptions. Such a gigantic task is necessarily of slow progress; nor can its advancement be counted by noses or ballots. It is the failure to realize fully the enormity of the task that is partly responsible for the pessimism that so often overtakes the active spirits of the movement. To that is added the lack of clarity regarding the manner of social accoutrements.

The Old is to give birth to the New. How do such things happen? as little Wendla asks her mother in Wedekind's *Frühlings Erwachen*. We have outgrown the stork of Social Revolution that will deliver us the newborn child of ready-made equality, fraternity, and liberty. We now conceive of the coming social life as a condition rather than a system. A condition of mind, primarily; one based on solidarity of interests arising from social understanding and enlightened self-interest. A system can be organized, made. A condition must be developed. This development is determined by existing environment and the intellectual tendencies of the times. The causation of both is no doubt mutual and interdependent, but the factor of individual and propagandistic effort is not to be underestimated.

The social life of man is a center, as it were, whence radiate numerous intellectual tendencies, crossing and zigzagging, receding and approaching each other in interminable succession. The points of convergence create new centers, exerting varying influences upon the larger center, the general life of humanity. Thus new intellectual and ethical atmospheres are established, the degree of their influence depending, primarily, on the active enthusiasm of the adherents; ultimately, on the kinship between the new ideal and the requirements of human nature. Striking this true chord, the new ideal will affect ever more intellectual centers which gradually begin interpreting themselves into life and transvaluing the values of the great general center, the social life of man.

Anarchism is such an intellectual and ethical atmosphere. With sure hand it has touched the heart of humanity, influencing the world's foremost minds in literature, art, and philosophy. It has resurrected the individual from the ruins of the social debacle. In the forefront of human advance, its progress is necessarily painfully slow: the leaden weight of ages of ignorance and superstition hangs heavily at its heels. But its slow progress should by no means prove discouraging. On the contrary: it evidences the necessity of greater effort, of solidifying existing libertarian centers, and of ceaseless activity to create new ones.

The immaturity of the past had blinded our vision to the true requirements of the situation. Anarchism was regarded, even by its adherents, as an ideal for the future. Its practical application to current life was entirely ignored. The propaganda was circumscribed by the hope of ushering in the Social Revolution. Preparation for the new social life was not considered necessary. The gradual development and growth of the coming day did not enter into revolutionary concepts. The dawn had been overlooked. A fatal error, for there is no day without dawn.

The martyrdom of Francisco Ferrer will not have been in vain if, through it, the Anarchists—as well as other radical elements—will realize that, in social as well as in individual life, conception precedes birth. The social conception which we need, and must have, is the creation of libertarian centers which shall radiate the atmosphere of the dawn into the life of humanity.

Many such centers are possible. But the most important of all is the young life, the growing generation. After all, it is they upon whom will devolve the task of carrying the work forward. Just in the proportion that the young generation grows more enlightened and libertarian, will we approach a freer society. Yet in this regard we have been, and still are, unpardonably negligent; we Anarchists, Socialists, and other radicals. Protesting against the superstition-breeding educational system, we nevertheless continue to subject our children to its baneful influence. We condemn the madness of war, yet we permit our offspring to be inculcated with the poison of patriotism. Ourselves more or less emancipated from false bourgeois standards, we still suffer our children to be corrupted by the hypocrisy of the established. Every such parent directly aids in the perpetuation of dominant ignorance and slavery. Can we indeed expect a generation reared in the atmosphere of the suppressive, authoritarian educational régime, to form the cornerstone of a free, self-reliant humanity? Such parents are criminally guilty toward themselves and their children: they rear the ghost that will divide their house against itself, and strengthen the bulwarks of darkness.

No intelligent radical can fail to realize the need of the rational education of the young. The rearing of the child must become a process of liberation by methods which shall not impose ready-made ideas, but which should aid the child's natural self-unfoldment. The purpose of such an education is not to force the child's adaptation to accepted concepts but to give free play to his originality, initiative, and individuality. Only by freeing education from compulsion and restraint can we create the environment for the manifestation of the spontaneous interest and inner incentives on the part of the child. Only thus can we supply rational conditions favorable to the development of the child's natural tendencies and his latent emotional and mental faculties. Such methods of education, essentially aiding the child's imitative quality and ardor for knowledge, will develop a generation of healthy intellectual independence. It will produce men and women capable, in the words of Francisco Ferrer, "of evolving without stopping, of destroying and renewing their environment without cessation; of renewing themselves also; always ready to accept what is best, happy in the triumph of new ideas, aspiring to live multiple lives in one life."

Upon such men and women rests the hope of human progress. To them belongs the future. And it is, to a very considerable extent, in our own power to pave the way. The death of Francisco Ferrer were in vain, our indignation, sympathy, and admiration worthless, unless we translate the ideals of the martyred educator into practice and life, and thus advance the human struggle for enlightenment and liberty.

A beginning has already been made. Several schools, along Ferrer lines, are being conducted in New York and Brooklyn; Philadelphia and Chicago are also about to open classes. At present the efforts are limited, for lack of aid and teachers, to Sunday schools. But they are the nucleus of grand, far-reaching potentiality. The radical elements of America, and chiefly the Francisco Ferrer Association, could rear no worthier nor more lasting monument to the memory of the martyred educator, Francisco Ferrer, than by a generous response to this appeal for the establishment of the first Francisco Ferrer Day School in America.

The Confession of a Convict

(The 19th of December, 1913, was "confession evening" at the "Twilight Club", New York, among whose members are the "best" people, supreme court judges, and other pillars of society. "Confessions" were made by a drunkard, a dope fiend, an actress, a labor agitator, a convict, etc., some of whom spoke in complete darkness, to hide their identity.)

This is an evening of confession, and I therefore at once confess myself a lawbreaker, a criminal — if you will — and a convict.

Mr. Chairman, Ladies and Gentleman, I beg your kind indulgence, for the convict's manner is uncouth, his speech ragged, his thoughts indecently naked. For only the convict, the outcast from the fold of commonplace respectability and dull conformity, can afford the luxury of frank, honest expression. And I should be honest with you — not only because of my lack of respect for that which is respected but the general consensus of stupidity, but rather because I hold in high respect my fellow convicts the world over, and — myself.

And I make my confession, not in the protecting shadow of cowardly darkness, but in the full glare of the challenging light which defies all sham and hypocrisy, however generally revered, and which is neither afraid nor ashamed of anything that is human.

And the convict, the criminal, Ladies and Gentlemen, is human. So human, indeed, that one of your great ethical teachers was compelled to cry out: "I have within me the capacity for every crime". Nor do I believe that Emerson merely said this as an abandonment of generosity, with the desire of uttering something great and levelling. I think he meant exactly what he said. For I believe that "within every bit of human flesh and spirit that has ever crossed the enigma bridge of life, from the prehistoric racial morning until now, all crime and all virtue were germinal." Out of the same stuff are we sprung, you and I and all of us, and if perchance in you the virtue has grown and not the vice, do not therefore conclude that you are essential different from him whom you have helped to put in stripes and behind bars. Your balance may be more even, you may be mixed in smaller proportions, or the outside temptation has not come upon you.

But has virtue really grown in you, and not vice? If the most respected and righteous among us, if our holiest and purist and better-than-thou pillars of church and state and society were for once to enter this confessional, in the frank abandon of their naked souls, would there be a single one left to cast and the first stone at the criminal and convict? Would there be any essential difference between the trust magnate and pick-pocket, except in the size of the booty they have stolen? Would there be any real difference between the great general or the judges on the criminal bench, and the ordinary murderer, except in the number of their victims? Would there be any difference between the employer of cheap labor or the Christian proprietor of a large department store, and the despicable creature we know has the cadet, except in the number of the girls they have forced into prostitution?

And whose crime is the greater—that of the man who steals my pocketbook or that of respected captains of industry who weave the very flesh and blood of their starving slaves into the luxury and license of the master's life?

Who is the real criminal, Ladies and Gentlemen? Is it the starveling who occasionally steals a loaf of bread or burglarizes my house or is it he who is the eternal vampire on the body of labor, forever feeding on the bone and marrow of the worker, exploiting and oppressing him, always keeping him on the verge of starvation that he may exercise his benevolent charity upon him, and ultimately degrading him to the lowest depths.

Thus is society organized, you'll say. Yes, thus: that a handful of the masters of life vampire upon the whole people. And therefore I indict modern society, this unholy union of authority and capital; I indict society as the greatest—aye, the only Criminal, the great universal crime that breeds and feeds the swamp of our whole social life with all its misery and degradation, all its evil and crimes.

For what is ordinarily called "crime" is but starvation. Ninety percent of all lawbreaking is of an economic nature. But it is not lawbreaking that makes the criminal. For as Oscar Wilde aptly said, "You may keep the law, and yet be worthless. You may break the law and yet be fine." It is starvation that fills our prisons. It is our wrong and unjust economic conditions that are the source of fully nine-tenths of all crime. And as to the other tenth—though a crime may not be against property, it may spring from misery and rage and depression produced by our perverted social conditions. Jealousy, itself, an extraordinary source of crime in modern life, is an emotion closely bound up with our conceptions of property. Abolish private property and the social robbery it involves, and you will have abolished the chief fountainhead of all crime and the spirit that generates it in human society.

And now, as to the criminal in our prisons and penitentiaries. Why, do you know, he is not to be found there. There you will indeed find men convicted of offenses against the law; but the real, bigger criminals, -- they are the large fish that break through the net of the law which is built to catch only the little fry.

The species "criminal" is a fiction of uncritical prejudice that deals only with theories, with imaginary abnormalities and aberrations. Through the obscure spectacles of preconceived notion and stubborn narrow-mindedness, men of the Lombroso stamp see only the "criminal species", entirely blind to the conception of crime as a social phenomenon, blind to the fact that the criminal, as an individual, is a unit of the larger species Man. The so-called criminal is not a little drop outside the ocean of life. He is one of us; his crime but the feverish pulse-beat of our sick social body.

The theory of the criminal species is at best but a cheap salve for the guilty social conscience. I suspect that if a good many respectable, decent, never-did-a-wrong-thing-in-their-lives people were to undergo the measurement test offered to the so-called "born criminal", malformed ears and disproportionately long thumbs would be equally found among them, if they took the precaution to represent themselves as criminals first.

I speak from experience. In my close association with criminals during fourteen years, in daily and hourly contact, not as an outsider, but as an equal — I have come to know them well and intimately. When I first came in touch with them, I entertained the idea of the criminal type, the species "criminal", a classification very much beloved by our prison reformists and criminologists. But closer contact and better understanding dispelled the fiction of the species and revealed the man, the individual, behind the convict.

There is no criminal type. In fact, the so-called criminal and convict is far more individualized, far more of a distinct personality than the average stupid citizen. He possesses a certain amount of initiative, considerable daring and independence of thought and action — traits, which, you will agree with me, are not the common earmarks of the average man. I have found no criminal type, but what I did find is that there are two classes of victims — the accidental and the professional. The accidental victim is the criminal by accident, one who has committed a crime as a result of some unusual combination of circumstances. The professional, on the other hand, is the one who follows crime as the ordinary pursuit of his life, similarly as the business man follows his profession of "stealing an honest living."

The line between these two classes is not drawn sharply nor is it a definite one. Very often the accidental victim, because of his prison experience and all it involves, is forced into the ranks of the professional. Now, what happens to the men who get into prison? What do we do to them? Do we try to call out their better nature by humane and kind treatment? Oh, no! My time is too limited to permit me to dwell on this matter, but everyone even slightly familiar with conditions in our penal institutions is aware that the whole system is built on the principle of revenge, of brutal humiliation and barbarous punishment. I need only refer to the blackjack, the dungeon, the bullring, the water cure, to give you an idea of the spirit dominant in those institutions. And no wonder. For the prison in the last analysis is the mirror of society at large, the perfect model of our social arrangement whose cornerstone is hypocrisy, deceit, oppression and injustice. Punishment is degrading, even more to the one wielding the whip than to his victim. The history of crime clearly demonstrates that the more punishment is inflicted, the more crime is produced. And after you have tortured the poor convict for several years, degraded him to the lowest, broken him in body and spirit, you turn him out into a cold world without money or friends, and with the stigma of "convict" burned into his very soul. Having embittered and demoralized him to the verge of desperation, you demand that he become a good and useful citizen.

Is it any wonder, then, that your prisons have proved to be veritable hot-houses of crime—for what is the ex-convict to do, with every one an Ishmael against him?

Your good police and detective departments will see to it that the ex-convict shall get no show. He will be speedily arrested on one pretext or another, and a kind Christian judge will decree that he be put away for a long term of years, for is it not his second offence?

Let us be done with all this sham and hypocrisy. Let us admit once and for all that crime is social; that our wrong economic conditions, by enriching the few at the cost of the many, are the true and only sources of crime. And let us emancipate ourselves from the stupid notion that the criminal is a being different or apart from the rest of us. There is no need of holding our skirts that he may not contaminate us. Indeed it is we who contaminate the criminal; it is we, society at large, that are guilty of far greater and more terrible crimes against the criminal than he has ever committed against us. In justice to him, and to ourselves, primarily, let us be honest, and brave enough to look the facts in the face; and if we are sincere in this matter, if we really and truly want to do away with the criminal and the convict, let us eradicate the causes of crime, rather than try hypocritically to patch up and hide our social sores.

The first step in reforming the criminal is to reform ourselves, for he is our brother, of the same blood and flesh. A more enlightened social attitude toward crime and criminals will serve to humanize, to some extent, our penal institutions, and will inject a little of the milk of kindness into the bitter cup of the convict. And the next step is to treat the cause instead of the effect. When you cease to justify and maintain present conditions of capitalistic exploitation and governmental oppression, and all other institutions based upon man's inhumanity to man, when honest men will realize their solidarity with the aspirations of labor for complete emancipation from all bondage, when Man will at last awaken from his nightmare of private ownership, of punishment and authority, then will crime and criminals forever disappear and make this earth fit for decent men and women to live in.

The Only Hope of Ireland

[Originally published in The Blast, vol.1, no.13, page 2; May 15, 1916]

Most Irishmen, in and out of Ireland, seem unanimous in condemning the brutality of the British government toward the leaders of the unsuccessful revolt.

There is no need to recite here the atrocious measures of repression practiced by England toward her subject races. The arrogant and irresponsible tyranny of the British government in this relation is a matter of history. The point of interest just now is, what did the Irish people, or at least the Sinn Feiners, expect England to do in the given circumstances?

I am not interested in the weak-kneed editors of Irish-American papers who bemoan, with all due decorum, Great Britain's "lack of generosity" in dealing with the captured Sinn Feiners, or who hide their cowardice by arguments about the "mistake" the British government has committed by its harsh methods.

It is disgusting to hear such rot. As a matter of fact, it is entirely in keeping with the character and traditions of the British government to show no quarter to rebels. Those familiar with the colonial history of Great Britain know that the English government and its representatives have systematically practiced the most heinous brutality and repression to stifle the least sign of discontent, in Ireland, in India, Egypt, South Africa—wherever British rapacity found a source of aggrandizement. Burning villages, destroying whole districts, shooting rebels by the wholesale, aye, even resorting to the most inhuman torture of suspects, as in the Southwestern

Punjab and other parts of India—these have always been the methods of the British government.

"The measures taken by us," said Sir Michael O'Dwyer, Governor of the province of Punjab, in his Budget speech in the Punjab Legislative Council, April 22, 1915, "have proven that the arm of the Sirkar (British government) is long enough to reach and strong enough to strike those who defy the law." The nature of this "long and strong arm" is clearly characterized by Lord James Bryce: "The English govern India on absolute principles. There is in British India no room for popular initiative or popular interference with the acts of the rulers, from the Viceroy down to the district official. Society in India is not an ordinary civil society. It is a military society, military first and foremost. The traveler feels himself, except perhaps in Bombay, surrounded by an atmosphere of gunpowder all the time he stays in India."

The Irish rebels and their sympathizers know all this. But what they don't know, or refuse to admit, is that these methods of suppressing discontent are not merely colonial policy. They have also been practiced by the English government at home, against its native sons, the English workers. Just now the iron hand of conscription is driving thousands of Great Britain's toilers into involuntary military servitude. Long terms of imprisonment are meted out to everyone having conscientious scruples against murder, to every anti-militarist protestant, and many have been driven to suicide rather than turn murderers of their fellowmen. The Irish people, like everyone else, ought to know that the claim of the English government of "protecting weaker nations and fighting for democracy" is the most disgusting hypocrisy ever dished up to a muttonhead public. Nor is the British government in this respect any better or worse than the governments of Kaiser, Czar or President. Government is but the shadow the ruling class of a country casts upon the political life of a given nation. And the priests of Mammon are always the ruling class, whatever the temporary label of the exploiters of the people.

We don't fool anyone by parroting that it was "a mistake" on the part of the British government to use the sternest methods against the Sinn Fein leaders. It was *not* a mistake. To the English government, to *any* government, the only safe rebel is a dead rebel. The ruthless shooting down of the insurrection leaders, the barbarous execution of James Connolly, who was severely wounded in the Dublin fighting and had to be propped with pillows that the soldiers could take good aim at him—all this may serve to embitter the Irish people. But unless that bitterness express itself in action, in reprisals—individual or collective—against the British government, the latter will have no cause to regret its severity. It is dangerous to let rebels live. If the Irish at home have no more spirit than the Irish in America, the English government has nothing to fear. The Irish-Americans are easily the most powerful influence in American political life. What have these Irish-Americans done to stop the atrocities of Great Britain? They have held mass meetings here and there to "protest" against the continuing executions of Sinn Feiners. They have sufficient political power in the country to cause President Wilson to call a halt to British atrocities, to force the English government to treat the Sinn Feiners as prisoners of war, which they are. But the Irish-American priests of Church and State would not dream of such drastic measures: politicians don't do that.

More effective yet it would have been if some member or members of the numerous Irish societies had captured a few representatives of the British government in this country as hostages for the Irish rebels awaiting execution. A British Consul ornamenting a lamppost in San Francisco or New York would quickly secure the respectful attention of the British lion. The British Ambassador, in the hands of Washington Irishmen, would more effectively petition his Majesty, King Edward, for the lives of the Irish rebel leaders than all the resolutions passed at mass meetings.

After all, it is the Redmonds and the Carsons who are chiefly responsible for the failure of the rebellion in Ireland. They were the first to condemn the "rash step" of a people for centuries enslaved and oppressed to the verge of utter poverty and degradation. Thus they in the very beginning alienated the support that the uprising might have received in and out of Ireland. It was this treacherous and cowardly attitude of the Irish home rule politicians that encouraged the English government to use the most drastic measures in suppressing the revolt.

May outraged Ireland soon learn that its official leaders are like unto all labor politicians: the lackeys of the rulers, and the very first to cry "Crucify!"

The hope of Ireland lies not in home rule, nor its leaders. It is not circumscribed by the boundaries of the Emerald Isle. The precious blood shed in the unsuccessful revolution will not have been in vain if the tears of their great tragedy will clarify the vision of the sons and daughters of Erin and make them see beyond the empty shell of national aspirations toward the rising sun of the international brotherhood of the exploited in all countries and climes combined in a solidaric struggle for emancipation from every form of slavery, political *and* economic revolution!

Friedrich Nietzsche

"There the gallows, rope and hooks And the hangman's beard is red; People 'round and poisoned looks, Nothing new and nothing dread!

"Know it well—from fifty sources Laughing in your face I cry: Would you hang me? Save your forces! Why hang me who cannot die!

"Beggars ye! who hate the tougher Man who holds the envied lot; True I suffer, true I suffer As to you—ye rot, ye rot!

"I am breath, dew, all resources, After fifty hangings, Why! Would you hang me? Save your forces! Would you kill me who cannot die!"

Deportation, Its Meaning and Menace: Last Message to the People of America

Ellis Island, New York, U.S.A., December, 1919.

The war is over, but peace there is not. On a score of fronts human slaughter is going on as before; men, women, and children are dying by the hundred thousands because of the blockade of Russia; the "small nations" are still under the iron heel of the foreign oppressor; Ireland, India, Egypt, Persia, Korea, and numerous other peoples, are being decimated and exploited even more ruthlessly than before the advent of the Great Prophet of World Democracy; "self-determination" has become a by-word, nay a crime, and world-wide imperialism has gotten a strangle hold upon humanity.

What, then, has the Great War accomplished? To what purpose the sacrifice of millions of human lives, the unnamable loss in blood and treasure? What, especially, has happened in these United States?

Fresh in mind are still the wonderful promises made in behalf of the War. It was to be the last war, a holy crusade of liberty against tyranny, a war upon all wars that was to sweep the earth clear of oppression and misery, and make the world safe for true democracy.

As with a sacred fire burned the heart of mankind. What soul so small, what human so low, not to be inspired by the glorious shibboleth of liberty and well-being for all! A tornado of social enthusiasm, a new-born world consciousness, swept the United States. The people were aflame with a new faith; they would slay the Dragon of Despotism, and conquer the world for democracy.

True, it was but yesterday their sovereign will registered a mighty protest against human slaughter and bloodshed. With a magnificent majority they had voted not to participate in the foreign War, not to become entangled in the treacherous schemes of European despotisms. Triumphantly they had elected as President of the United States the man who "kept them out of the war" that he might still keep them out of it.

Then suddenly, almost over night, came the change. From Wall Street sounded the bugle ordering the retreat of Humanity. Its echo reverberated in Washington, and thence throughout the whole country. There began a campaign of war publicity that roused the tiger in man and fed his lust for blood and vengeance. The quiet, made the villain of the wildest stories of "enemy" atrocities and outrages. The nation-wide propaganda of hatred, persecution, and intolerance carried its subtle poison into the hearts of the obscurest hamlet, and the minds of the people were systematically confused and perverted by rivers of printer's ink. The conscience of America. wanting peace, was stifled in the folds of the national emblem, and its voice drowned by the martial beat of a thousand war drums.

Here and there a note of protest was heard. Radicals of various political and social faiths—Anarchists, Socialists, I.W.Ws., some pacifists, conscientious objectors, and other anti-militarists sought to stem the tide of the war hysteria. They pointed out that the people of the United States had no interest in the European War. That this country, because of its geographical location and natural advantages, was beyond all danger of invasion. They showed that the War was the result of European over-preparedness for war, aggravated by a crisis in capitalist competition, old monarchical rivalries, and ambitions of super-despotic rulers. The peoples of Europe, the radicals emphasized, had neither say nor interest in the war: they were the sheep led to slaughter on the altar of Mammon contending against Baal. America's great humanitarian mission, the war protestants insisted, was to keep out of the war, and use its potent influence and compelling economic and financial power to terminate the European slaughter and bring peace to the bleeding nations of die old world.

But these voices of sanity and judgment were lost in the storm of unloosed war passions. The brave men and women that dared to speak in behalf of peace and humanity, that had the surpassing integrity of remaining true to themselves and to their ideals, with the courage of facing danger and death for conscience sake—these, the truest friends of Man, had to bear the cross of Golgotha, as did the Nazarene of yore, as the lovers of humanity have done all through the centuries of human progress. The jail and lynch law for them; execution and persecution by their contemporaries. But if it be true that history repeats itself, surely these political "criminals" of today will be hailed tomorrow as martyrs and pioneers.

The popular war hysteria was roused and especially successfully cultivated by the alleged progressive, "intellectual" element in the United States. Their notoriously overwhelming self-esteem and vanity had been subtly flattered by their fellow intellectual, the college professor become President. This American intelligentzia inclusive of a good many quite unintelligent suffragettes, was the real "balance of power" in the re-election of Woodrow Wilson.

The silken cord (occasionally golden in spots) of mutual interests that bound the President and the intellectual element ultimately proved much stronger at their end that at his. The feeling of gratitude is always more potent with the giver than with the recipient. Howbeit the "liberals", the "radicals", were devoted heart and soul to the professor, they stood solidly behind the President, to use their own intellectually expressive phrase.

Shame upon the mighty power of the human mind! It was the "radical intellectuals" who, as a class, turned traitors to the best interests of humanity, perverted their calling and traditions, and became the bloodiest canines of Mars. With a power of sophistry that the Greek masters of false logic never matched, they cited history, philosophy, science—aye, they called their very Christ to witness that the killing of man by man is a most worthy and respectable occupation, indeed a very Christian institution, and that wholesale human slaughter, if properly directed and successfully conducted, is a very necessary evolutionary factor, a great blessing in disguise.

It was this "intellectual" element that by perversion of the human mind turned a peace-demanding people into a war-mad mob. The popular refusal to volunteer for Service was hailed by them as a universal demand for military draft as "the most democratic expression of a free citizenship." Forced service became in their interpretation "equality of contribution for rich and poor alike." The protest of one's conscience against killing was branded by them as high treason, and even mere disagreement regarding the causes of the war, or the slightest criticism of the administration, was condemned as disloyalty and pro-Germanism. Every expression of humanity, of social sympathy, and understanding was cried down with a Babel of high phrases, in which "patriotism" and democracy" competed in volume. Oh, the tragedy of the human mind that absorbs fine words and empty phrases, and is deaf to motives and blind to deeds!

Yet there lacked unanimity in the strenuously cultivated war demand. There was no popular enthusiasm for American participation in the European holocaust. Mothers protested against their children being torn from the home hearth; fathers hid their sons. The spirit of discontent was abroad. The Government had to resort to drastic methods: the hand of white terror was lifted in Washington. Again we raised our voices to warn the people, the revolutionists of various social views who remained true to our ideal of human brotherhood and proletarian solidarity. We pointed out that the masses of the world had nothing to gain and everything to lose by war; that the chief sufferers of every war were the workers, and that they were being used as mere pawns in the game of international diplomacy and imperialist capitalism. We reminded the toilers that they alone possessed the power to wage war or make peace, and that they — as the creators of the world's wealth — were the true arbiters of the fate of humanity. Their mission, we reiterated, is to secure peace on earth, and the product of labor to the producers.

Emphatically we warned the people of America against the policy of suppression by the enactment of special legislation. Alleged war necessity was being used — we asserted — to incorporate in the statute books new laws and new legal principles that would remain operative after the war, and be effective for the continued prohibition of governmentally unapproved thoughts and views. The practice of stifling and choking free speech and press, established and tolerated during the war, sets a most dangerous precedent for after-war days. The principle of such outrages upon liberty once introduced, it will require a long and arduous struggle to win back the liberties lost. "Eternal vigilance is the price of liberty." Thus we argued.

Here again the "intellectuals" and radicals of chameleon hue hastened to the rescue of the forces of reaction. We were scoffed at, our "vain fears" ridiculed. It was all for the best interests of the country-the sophists protested-for the greater security and glory of Democracy.

Now reaction is in full swing. The actual reality is even darker than our worst predictions. Liberty is dead, and white terror on top dominates the country. Free speech is a thing of the past. Not a city in the whole wide land but that forbids the least expression of an unpopular opinion. It is descriptive of the whole situation that after thirty years' activity in New York, we are unable—upon our return from prison—to secure any hall, large or small, to lecture even on the subject of prison life or to speak on the question of amnesty for political and industrial prisoners. The doors of every meeting place are closed to us, as well as to other revolutionists, by order of the powers that be.

Free press has been abolished, and every radical paper that dares speak out is summarily suppressed. Raids of public gatherings, of offices, and private dwelling places, accomplished with utmost brutality and uncalled for violence, are of daily occurrence throughout the United States. The headquarters of Anarchists, of Socialists, of I.W.W.s, of the Union of Russian Workers, and numerous other progressive and educational organizations, have been raided by the local police and Federal agents in practically every city of this country. Men and women are beaten up indiscriminately, fearfully clubbed and blackjacked without any provocation, frequently to be released afterwards because no offence whatever could be charged against them. Books and whole libraries of "radical centers" are confiscated, even text books of arithmetic or geography torn to shreds, furniture destroyed, pianos and victrolas smashed to kindling wood—all in the name of the new Democracy and for the safety of the glorious, free Republic of these United States.

The half-baked radicals, their hearts as soft as their heads, now stand aghast at this terrible sight. They had helped to win the war. Some had sacrificed fathers, brothers, husbands—all of them had suffered an agony of misery and tears, to help the cause of humanity, to make the world safe for democracy. Is this what we fought and bled for? they are asking. Have we been misled by the fine-sounding phrases of a Professor, and have we in turn helped to delude the people, the suffering masses of the world? Is the great prophet of the New Democracy strong only in rhetoric?

Pity the mind that awaits miracles and looks expectantly to a universal Savior. The clear-sighted man, well informed, may reasonably foresee the inevitability of certain results from given causes. But only a charlatan can play the great Savior, and only the fool has faith in him. Individuals, however great, may profoundly influence, but are powerless to control, the fate of mankind. Deep socio-political causes produced the war. The Kaiser did not create it, though the spirit of Prussianism no doubt accelerated its coming. Nor is President Wilson responsible for the present bloody peace. He did not make the war: he was made by it. He did not make the peace: he was unmade by it. The social and economic forces that control the world are stronger than any man, than any set of men. These forces are inherent in the fundamental institutions of our wage-slave civilization, in the social atmosphere created by it, and in the individual mind. These forces are by no means harmonious. The human heart and mind, eternally reaching out for greater joy and beauty—the spirit of idealism, in short—is constantly at strife with the established, the institutionalized. These contending social and human factors produce war, as they produce revolution.

The powers that succeeded in turning the instinctive current of man's idealism into the channels of war, became the masters of human destiny for the nonce. By a campaign of publicity and advertising on a scale history had never witnessed before, by chicanery and lying, by exaggeration and misrepresentation, by persistent and long-continued appeals to the basest as well as to the noblest traits of man, by every imaginable and unprecedented manner and method, the great financial interests, eager for war and aided by the international Junkers, thrust humanity into the great world war. Whatever of noble impulse and unsophisticated patriotism there was in the hearts of the masses, in and out of uniform, was soon almost totally drained in the fearsome rivers of human blood, in the brutal, filthy, degrading charnel house of elemental passions set on fire. But the tiger in man, once thoroughly awakened, grew strong and more vicious with the sights he witnessed and the food he was fed on. The basest propensities unchained, the anti-social tendencies engendered and encouraged by the war, and the war propaganda, are now let loose upon the country. Hatred, intolerance, persecution and suppression — the efficient "educational" factors in the preparedness and war campaign — are now permeating the very heart of this country and propagating its virulent poison into every phase of our social life.

But there is no more "Hun" to be hated and lynched. Commerce and business know their interests. We must feed Germany at a good profit. We must do business with its people. Exit the Hun-*der Moor hat seine Schuldigkeit gethan*. What a significant side-light on the artificiality and life-brevity of national and racial antagonisms, when the fires of mutual distrust and hatred are not fed by the interested stokers of business and religion! But the Frankenstein and intolerance and suppression cultivated by the war campaign is there, alive and vital, and must find some vent for his accumulated bitterness and misery.

Or, there, the radical, the Bolshevik! What better prey to be cast to the Frankenstein monster?

The powers that be — the plutocratic imperialist and the jingo profiteer — all heave a happy sigh of relief.

The after-war conditions in the United States are filling the Government and the more intelligent, class-conscious capitalists with trepidation. Revolution is stalking across Europe. Its specter is threatening America. Disquieting signs multiply daily. A new discontent, boding ill and full of terrible possibilities, is manifest in every walk of life. Ile war has satisfied no one. Only too obviously the glorious promises failed of fulfillment. Excepting the great financial interests and some smaller war profiteers, the American people at large are aching with a poignant disappointment.

Some vaguely, other more consciously and clearly, but almost all feel themselves in some way victimized. They had brought supreme sacrifices, suffered untold misery and pain, in the confident hope of a great change to come into their lives after the victorious war, in the assurance of a radically changed and bettered world.

The people feel cheated. Not yet have they been able to fix their gaze definitely upon the specific source of their disappointments, to define the true causes of their discontent. But their impatience with existing conditions is passionate and bitter, and their former faith in the established order profoundly shaken. Significant symptoms of a social breakdown! Revolutions begin in the heart and in the mind. Action follows in due course. Political and industrial institutions, bereft of the people's faith in them, are doomed. The changed attitude toward the once honored and sacred conditions, now evident throughout the land, symbolizes the complete bankruptcy of the existing order. The old conceptions and ideas underlying present-day society are fast disintegrating. New ideals are germinating in the hearts of the masses—a prolific soil, rich with the promise of a brighter future. America is on the threshold of the Social Revolution.

All this is well realized by the financial and political masters of this country. The situation is profoundly disquieting. But most terrifying to them is the new attitude of labor. It is unprecedented, intolerable in its complete disregard of long accepted standards and conditions, its open rebellion against Things As They Are, its "shameless demands," its defiance of constituted authority. Is it possible, the masters wonder, that we had gone too far in our wartime promises of democracy and freedom, of justice to the workers, of well-being for all? Too reckless was our motto, "Labor will win the war": it has given the toilers a sense of their power, it has made them arrogant, aye, menacing. No more are they satisfied with "a fair day's wage for a fair day's work"; no, not even with wages doubled and trebled. They are laying sacrilegious hands upon the most sacrosanct institution of private ownership, they challenge the exclusive mastery of the owner in his own mine and mill, they demand actual participation in industry, even in the most secret councils that control production and manipulate distribution they even dare suggest the taking over by labor of all industry.

Unheard of impudence! Yet this is not all. More menacing still is the revolutionary spirit that is beginning to transfuse itself through every rank of labor, from the highest-paid to the lowest, organized and the unorganized as well. Disobedience is rampant.

Gone is the good old respect for orders, the will of superiors is secretly thwarted or openly defied, the mystic power of contracts has lost its old hold. Labor is in rebellion—in rebellion against State and Capital, aye, even against their own leaders that have a so long held them in check.

No time is to be lost! Quick, drastic action is necessary. Else the brewing storm will overwhelm us, and the workers deprive us of the wealth we have been at such pains to accumulate. Even now there are such terribly disquieting rumblings, as if the very earth were shaking beneath our feet—rumors of "the dictatorship of the proletariat," of "Soviets of workers, soldiers and sailors." Horrible thought! Why, if the soldiers should join these discontented workers, what would become of us poor capitalists? Indeed, have, not the police of Boston already set the precedent—made common cause with labor, these traitors to their masters!

"Soviet of workers," "dictatorship of the Proletariat"! Why, that's the Russian idea, the terrible Bolshevik menace. Never shall this, the most heinous crime, be forgiven Soviet Russia! Readily would we overlook their repudiation of the Czar's numerous obligations and even their refusal to pay their debts to the American and European moneylenders. We'd find some way to recuperate our losses, at a reasonable profit, maybe. But that they have broken down the very pillars of capitalism, abolished profits, given to the peasants the masters' lands for cultivation and use, proclaimed all wealth common property, and subjected the aristocrat and capitalist to the indignity of working for a living—this hellish arch-crime they shall never be forgiven.

That such things should threaten the rich men of this free country is intolerable. Nothing must be left undone to prevent such a calamity. It would be terrible to be put on a level with the common laborer, and we with all our millions unable to procure champagne, because, forsooth, some hod-carrier's brat—illegitimate, perchance— did not get his milk for breakfast. Unthinkable! That is chaos, anarchy! We must not permit our beloved country to come to such a pass. Labor rebellion and discontent must be crushed, energetically, forthwith. Bolsheviks ways and Soviet ideas must gain no foothold in America. But the thing must be done diplomatically; the workers must not be permitted to look into our cards. We should he strong as a lion, subtle as the snake.

The war-time anti-Hun propaganda is now directed against the "Bolshevik," "the radical," and particularly against the Slav or anything resembling him. The man or woman of Russian birth or nationality is made the especial target. The press, the pulpit, all the servile tools of capitalism and imperialism combine to paint Russia, Soviet Russia, in colors of blood and infamy. No misrepresentation, no lie too base to be flung at Russia. Falsehood and forgery the weapons where guns and bayonets have failed. The direct result of this poison propaganda is now culminating in American pogroms against Russians, Bolsheviks, communists, radicals, and progressives in general.

The United States has fortunately always been free from the vicious spirit of race hatred and persecution of the foreigner. The native negro excepted, this country has known no race problem. The American people were never guilty of harboring bitterness or deep-seated prejudice against members of other nationalities. In truth, the great majority of them are themselves of foreign birth or descent, the only true native being the American Indian. Whatever racial differences there may exist between the various nationalities or stocks, they have never assumed the form of active strife. On the contrary, they have always been of a superficial nature, due to misunderstanding or other temporary causes, and have never manifested themselves in anything save light, good-humored banter. Even the much-advertised antagonism of the West toward the Chinese and Japanese is not due to any inherent hatred, but rather to very definite commercial and industrial factors. In the case of the Russians especially, as well as in regard to members of the various branches of the Slavic race, the people of America have always been particularly friendly and well-disposed. But suddenly all the war-time hatred toward the "Hun enemy," the blindest intolerance and persecution, are poured upon the head of the Russian, the Slav. Great indeed is the power of propaganda! Great is the power of the American thought controller-the capitalist press. The Russian has become the victim of American pogroms!

Often and again in the past have we Anarchists pointed out that the feudal lords of this land would follow, in their march to imperialism, in the footsteps of the Czars of old Russia, and even outdo their preceptors. Our liberal friends denounced us as fanatics, alarmists, and pessimists. Yet now we are confronted with a state of affairs in democratic America which, in point of brutality and utter repudiation of every fundamental libertarian principle, surpasses the worst autocratic methods the Czars of Russia ever dared apply against political dissenters.

The world is familiar with the story of the pogrom horrors practiced upon the Jews of Czarist Russia. But what the world, especially the American world, does not know is that every pogrom in Russia was directly incited, financed, and prepared by the Government as a means of distracting the attention of the Russian people from the corrupt despotic regime under which they suffered — a deliberate method of confusing and checking the fast growing discontent and holding back the rising tide of revolutionary upheaval.

But thoughtful people in Russia were not long deceived by this hell's stratagem. That is why Russians of character and intelligence never lent themselves to the practice of Jew-baiting and persecution. The authorities frequently had to resort to importing the human dregs of distant communities, fill them with vodka, and then turn them loose on the defenseless Jews. These Black Hundreds and hooligans of Czarist Russia were the infamous regime now forever cast into the abyss of oblivion by the awakened and regenerated spirit of New Russia. There have been no pogroms in Soviet Russia.

But the Black Hundreds and the hooligans have now come to life again — in democratic America. Here they are more mad and pernicious than their Russian colleagues in crime had ever been. Their wild orgies of assault and destruction are directed, not against the Jew, but against the more comprehensive scapegoat of Capitalism, "the alien," the "radical." These are being made the lightning rod upon which is to be drawn all the fury of the storm that is menacing the American plutocracy. As the Czars pointed at the Jew as the sole source and cause of the Russian people's poverty and servitude, so the feudal lords of America have chosen the "foreign radical ... the Bolshevik" as the vicarious victim for the sins of the capitalist order. But while no intelligent and self-respecting Russian ever degraded himself with the Czar's bloody work, we see in our democracy so-called cultured people, professional men and women, "good Americans," inspired and aided by the "respectable, reputable" press, turn into bestial mobs. We see high Government officials, State and Federal, play the part of the hooligans encouraging and aiding the American Black Hundred of legionaries, in a frenzied crusade against the "foreigner," whose sole crime consists in taking seriously the American guarantees of free speech, free press, and free assembly.

The war hate against everything German was vicious enough, though the people of America were repeatedly assured that we were not making war against the German people. One can understand also, though not countenance, the vulgar clamor against the best and finest expressions of German culture, the stupid prohibition of the language of Goethe and Schiller, of the revolutionary music of Wagner and Beethoven, the poetry of Heine, the writings of Nietzsche, and all the other great creative works of Teuton genius. But what possible reason is there for the post-war hatred toward aliens in general and Russians in particular? The outrages and cruelties perpetrated upon Germans in America during the war pale almost into insignificance compared with the horrible treatment the Russians in the United States are now subjected to. In fact, the Czarist pogroms, barring a few exceptions, never rivaled the fearful excesses now happening almost daily in various American cities, their victims, men and women, guilty only of being Russians.

This state of affairs is the more significant because Russians, and the Slavic people in general, were hitherto always welcomed to these shores as the best offering Europe contributed to the Moloch of American industry. The Slav was so good natured, and docile, such a patient slave, so appreciative of the liberties he enjoyed in the new land — "liberties" which the socially conscious American had long since learned to see as a delusion and a snare. But to the unsophisticated Russian peasant, always half-starved and browbeaten, they seemed real and resplendent, the symbol of paradise found. By the thousands he flocked to the promised land, swarmed into the centers of industry to build our railroads, forge iron, dig coal, till the soil, weave cloth, and toil at scores of other useful occupations, his reward a mere pittance.

Nor was it only the workers in fields and factories who were welcomed here from Russia. Russian culture was an honored guest in America. The great literature of the Slav, his music, his dancing — all found the most generous reception and fullest appreciation. Above all, the Russian intelligentzia, the political refugees, exiles, and active revolutionists that came to America, and came — most of them — not merely to express their opinions but rather to plot the forcible overthrow of the Russian autocracy, all found sympathetic hearing and generous purses in this country, aye, even at the seat of Government.

And now? Now it is considered the most heinous crime to have been born in Russia.

What has caused this peculiar change? What is back of this sudden reversal of feeling?

It is the Russian Revolution. Not, of course, the Miliukov-Kerensky revolution, but the real revolution that gave birth to Soviet Russia. The submissive, enslaved, long-suffering Russian people unexpectedly transformed into a free, daring Giant breaking a new path for the progress of mankind—that is the reason for the changed attitude of the capitalistic world. It is one thing to help Russian revolutionists to overthrow the Czar and to put in his place a "democratic" form of government which has proven such a boon to our own Czars of commerce and industry. But it is quite a different thing to see the Prometheus of labor rise in his might, strike off his chains, and with the full consciousness of his complete economic power bring to life the dreams and aspirations of a thousand years, the economic, political, and spiritual emancipation of the masses of the world. This pioneer social experiment now being tried in Russia—the greatest and most fundamental ever witnessed in all history—is the guiding star to all the oppressed and disinherited of the world. Already its magic light is spreading over the whole European horizon, the harbinger of the approaching Dawn of Man. What if it should traverse the ocean and embrace our own shores within its orbit? The whole social order of the financial Czars, industrial Kaisers, and land Barons of America is at stake: the "order" maintained by club and gun, by jail and lynch law in and out of court; the "order" founded on robbery and violence, built upon sham and unreason, artificiality and insanity, and supported by misery and starvation, by the water cure, the dungeon and straitjacket; an "order" that transcends all chaos and daily makes confusion worse confounded.

Such social "order" is doomed. It bears within itself the virus of disintegration. Already the conscience of America is awakening. The war marked the crisis. Already American men have chosen imprisonment, torture, and death, rather than become participants in an unholy war. Already American men and women are beginning to realize the anti-social destructive character and purpose of authority and government by violence, force, and fraud. Already the workers of America are outgrowing the vicious circle of craft unionism, learning the lesson and the power of solidarity of the international proletariat, and gaining confidence in their own initiative and judgment, to the confusion and terror of their antiquated, spineless leadership. Already they are seeing through the sham of "equality before the law," and are in open rebellion to government by injunction.

A spark from the glowing flame of Soviet Russia, and the purse-proud autocracy of America may be swept away by the social conflagration.

Wherefore the united chorus of all Czars and Kaisers, "Death to the Bolsheviks, the aliens, the I.W.Ws., the Communists, the Anarchists!"

Whatever might be said of the American plutocracy and the Government, no one can accuse them of originality. The methods used by them to confuse and confound the people are but cheap imitations of the old tactics long resorted to by the despotic rulers of Europe. Even before the World War, Washington had borrowed many a trick from London. And all through the war American militarism, with its conscription, espionage, torture of conscientious objectors, and suppressive legislation, was but aping—stupidly and destructively—the modus operandi of the bankrupt imperialism of the Old World. For lack of originality and ideas, American officialdom was content to be the echo of the military and court circles of London and Paris. And now again we witness Washington following in the exact footsteps of the worst autocracy of modern times. For the hue and cry against the "alien" is a faithful replica of the persecution of the Jews by the Czars of Russia, and the American pogroms against radicals are the exaggerated picture of Russian Jew-baiting.

And, finally, the most infamous and most inhuman method of Czarist Russia, the method that sacrificed hundreds of thousands of the finest and bravest men and women of Russia, and systematically robbed the country of the very flower of its youth, is now being transplanted on American soil, in these great United States, the freest democracy on earth. The dreaded Russian administrative process the newest American institutions! Sudden seizure, anonymous denunciation, star chamber proceedings, the third degree, secret deportation and banishment to unknown lands. O shades of Jefferson, Thomas Paine, and Patrick Henry! That you must witness the bloodiest weapon of Czarism rescued from the ruins of defunct absolutism and introduced into the country for whose freedom you had fought so heroically!

What means the administrative process?

It means the suppression and elimination of the political protestant and social rebel. It is the practice of picking men upon the street, on the merest suspicion of "political untrustworthiness," of arresting them in their club rooms or homes, tearing them away from their families, locking them up in jails or detention pens, holding them incommunicado for weeks and months, depriving them of a hearing in open court, denying them trial by jury, and finally deporting them or banishing them to unknown shores. All this, not for any crime committed or even any punishable act charged, but merely on the denunciation of an enemy or the irresponsible accusation by a Secret Service man that the "suspect" holds certain unpopular or "forbidden" opinions.

Lest the truth or accuracy of this statement be called in question, let it be stated that at this very moment there are one hundred such "political suspects" held at Ellis Island, with several hundred more in the various Immigration Detention jails, every one of them a victim of the administrative process described above. Not one of them is charged with any specific crime; one and all are accused of entertaining "illegal" views on political or Social questions. Nearly all of them have been seized on the street or arrested in their homes or reading-rooms while engaged in the dangerous pursuit of studying the English language, mathematics, or American history. (The latter seems lately to be regarded by the authorities as a particularly dangerous occupation, and those guilty of it a prima facie menace to our American institutions.) Others were arrested in the factory, at their work bench, or in the numerous recent raids of homes and peaceful meetings. Many of them were beaten and clubbed most brutally, the wounds of some necessitating hospital treatment in the police stations they were subjected to the third degree, threatened, tortured, and finally thrust into the bull pens of Ellis Island. Here they are treated as dangerous felons, kept all the time under lock and key, and allowed to see their wives and families only once a week, with a screen between them and malicious guards constantly at their side. Here their mail is subjected to the most stringent censorship, and their letters delivered or not, according to the whims of the petty officials in charge. Here some of them, because they dared protest against their isolation and the putrid food, were placed in the insane asylum. Here it was that the brutal treatment and unbearable conditions of existence drove men and women, the politicals awaiting deportation, to the desperate extremity of a hunger strike, the last resort of defenseless beings, the paradoxical self-defense of despair. For weeks and months these men have now been kept prisoners at Ellis Island, tortured by the thought of their wives and children whom the Government has ruthlessly deprived of support, and living in constant uncertainty of the fate that is awaiting them, for the good American Government, refinedly cruel, is keeping their destination secret, and certain death may be the goal of the deportees when the hour of departure finally strikes.

Such is the treatment and the fate of the first group of Russian refugees from American "democracy." Such is the process known as the administrative methods, penalizing governmentally unapproved Thought, suppressing disbelief in the omniscience of the powers that be.

In enlightened, free America. Not in Darkest Russia.

When the terrible significance of the administrative process practiced in Russia became known in Europe, civilization stood aghast. It caused a storm of protest in the British Parliament, and called forth violent interpellations in the Italian Diet and the French Chamber. Even the German Reichstag, in the days of the omnipotent Kaiser, ventured a heated debate of the barbaric administrative process which doomed thousands of innocents to underground dungeons and the frozen taigas of Siberia.

Are the Czar's methods, the Third Section, the secret political spy organizations, anonymous denunciations, star chamber proceedings, deprivation of trial, wholesale deportations and banishment, to become an established American institution? Let the people speak.

The full significance of the principle of deportation is becoming daily more apparent. The field of its menace is progressively broadening. Not only the alien social rebel is to be crushed by the new White Terror. Its hand is already reaching out far for the naturalized American whose social views are frowned upon by the Government. And yet deeper it strikes. One hundred percent Americanism is to root out the last vestige, the very memory, of traditional American freedom. Not alone foreigners, but the naturalized citizen and the native-born are to be mentally fumigated, made politically "reliable" and governmentally kosher, by eliminating the social critics and industrial protestants, by denaturalization and banishment, by exile to the Island of Guam or to Alaska, the future Siberia of the United States.

Following the "alien radical," the naturalized American is the first victim of the Czarification of America. Patriotic profiteers and political hooligans are united in the cry for the "Americanization" of the foreigner in the United States. He is to be "naturalized," intellectually sterilized and immunized to Bolshevism, so that he may properly appreciate the glorious spirit of American democracy. Simultaneously, however, the Federal Government is introducing the new policy of summarily depriving the naturalized American of his citizenship, in order to bring him when so desired, within the scope of the administrative process which subjects the victim to deportation without trial.

A most important precedent had already been act. The case of Emma Goldman affords significant proof to what lengths the Government will go to rid itself of a disquieting social rebel, though he be a citizen for a quarter of a century.

The story is interesting and enlightening. More than eight years ago Secret Service men of the Federal Government were ordered to gather "material" in Rochester, N. Y., or elsewhere, that would enable the authorities to disfranchise a certain Rochester citizen. The man in question was of no concern whatever to Washington, as subsequent events proved. He was an ordinary citizen, a quiet working man, without any interest in social or political questions. He was never known to entertain any unpopular views or opinions. As a matter of fact, the man had long been considered dead by his local friends and acquaintances; since he had disappeared from his home years previously and no clue to his whereabouts or any sign that he was still among the living could be found; indeed, has not been found till this day, notwithstanding the best efforts. At great expense, and with considerable winking at its own rules and regulations in such matters, the United States Government finally disfranchised the man—the corpse, perhaps, for anything known to the contrary. The proceeding necessitated a good deal of secrecy and subterfuge, for even the wife of the man in question, whose status as citizen by right of her marriage was involved, was not apprised by the Government of its intended action. On the pretext that the man was not fully of legal age at the time of his naturalization 20 years before, the mighty Republic of America declared the citizenship of the man of unknown whereabouts and against whom no crime or offence of any kind was ever charged, as null and void.

Ten years passed. The disfranchised citizen, so far as humanly known, was still as dead as at the time of his denaturalization. No trace of him could be found, and nothing more was heard of the motives and purposes of the Government in depriving of citizenship a man who had apparently been dead for years. Dark and peculiar are the ways of Government.

More time passed. Then it became known that the United States Government intended to deport Emma Goldman. But Emma Goldman had acquired citizenship by marriage 30 years before, and, as a citizen, she could not be deported under the present laws of the United States. But lo and behold! The Government suddenly announced that Emma Goldman was a citizen no more, because her husband had been disfranchised ten years ago!

Dark and peculiar indeed are the ways of government. But there is Method in its madness.

What a striking comment this case afford on the true character Of government, and the chicanery and subterfuge it resorts to when legal means fail to achieve its purposes. Long did the United States Government bide its time. The moment was not propitious to get rid of Emma Goldman. But she must be gotten rid of, by fair means or foul. Yet public sentiment was not ready for such things as deportation and banishment. Patience! The hour of a great popular hysteria will come, will be made, if necessary, and then we shall deport this *bete noir* of government.

The moment has now come. It is here. The national hysteria against radicals, inspired and fed by the bourgeois press, pulpit, and politicians, has created the atmosphere needed to introduce in America the principle and practice of banishment. At last the Government may deport Emma Goldman, for through the width and breadth of the country there is not a Judge—and possibly not even a jury—with enough integrity and courage to give this enfant terrible a fair hearing and an unprejudiced examination of her claim to citizenship.

Therefore Emma Goldman is to be deported.

But her case sets a precedent, and American life is ruled by legal precedents. Henceforth the naturalized citizen may be disfranchised, on one pretext or another, and deported because of his or her social views and opinions. Already Congress is preparing to embody this worthy precedent in our national legislation by passing special laws providing for the disenfranchisement of naturalized Americans for reasons satisfactory to our autocratic regime.

Thus another link is forged to chain the great American people. For it is against the liberties and welfare of the people at large that these new methods are fundamentally directed. Not merely against Emma Goldman, the Anarchists, the I.W.W's., Communists, and other revolutionists. These are but the primary victims, the prologue which introduces and shadows forth the tragedy about to be enacted.

The ultimate blow of the imperialist plutocracy of America is aimed at Labor, at the increasing discontent of the masses, their growing class-consciousness, and their progressive aspiration for more joy and life and beauty. The fate of America is in the balance.

That is the true meaning and the real menace of the principle of deportation, banishment, and exile, now being introduced in the life of the United States. That is the purpose of the State and Federal Anti-Anarchist laws, criminal-syndicalist legislation, and all similar weapons that the master class is forging for the defeat of the awakening proletariat of America.

Shall the United States, once the land of opportunity, the refuge of all the oppressed, be Prussianized, Czarified? Shall the melting pot of the world be turned into a fiery caldron brewing strife and slaughter, spitting tyranny and assassination? Shall we here, on this soil baptized with the sacred blood of the great heroes of the Revolutionary War, engage in the sanguinary struggle of brother against brother? Shall we re-enact in this land the frightful nightmare of Darkest Russia? Shall this land re-echo the horrible tramp, tramp of a thousand feet, on their way to an American Siberia? Tortured bodies, manacled hands, clanking chains, in weary, endless procession-shall that be the heritage of our youth? Shall the songs of mothers be turned into a dirge, and little babies be suckled with the teat of hate?

No, it shall not be. There is yet time to pause, to turn back. High time, high time for the voice of every true man and woman, of every lover of liberty, to thunder forth such a mighty collective protest that shall reverberate from North to South, and East to West, and rouse the awakened manhood of America to a heroic stand for Liberty and Justice.

But if not, if our warning prediction unhappily come true and the fearful tragedy be played to its end, yet shall we not despair, nor misdoubt the finale.

Hateful is the Dream of Oppression. And as vain. Where the man who could name the judges that doomed Socrates? Where the persecutors of the Gracchi, the banishers of Aristides, the excommunicators of Spinoza and Tolstoy? Their very memory is obliterated by the footsteps of Progress. Unceasingly it marches, forward and upward, all obstacles notwithstanding, keeping time with the heart beats of Humanity. Vain the efforts to halt it, to banish ideas, to strangle thought. Vain the frenzied struggle to turn back the hands of Time. The mightiest Goliath of Reaction has fought his last fight-his final gesture, Old Russia, a hopeless surrender. Too late to revive this corpse. It is beyond resurrection. Attempts there may be, aye, will be, for the Bourbons never learn, and the people are long suffering. But attempts useless, destructive, utterly fatal to their purpose. The Dream of Reaction ends in abysmal nightmare.

It is darkest before dawn, in history as in nature. But the dawn has begun. In Russia. Its light is a promise and the hope of the world.

What's To Be Done?

Men and women of America, there is much work to be done. If you hate injustice and tyranny, if you love liberty and beauty, there is work for you. If oppression rouses your indignation, and the sight of misery and ugliness makes you unhappy, there is work for you. If your country is dear to you and the people your kin, there is work for you. There is much to be done.

Whoever you are, artist or educator, writer or worker—be you but a true man or true woman—there is important work for you. Let not prejudice and narrow-mindedness blind you. Let not a false press mislead you. Permit not this country to sink to the depths of despotism. Do not stand supinely by, while every passing day strengthens reaction. Rouse yourself and others to resent injustice and every outrage on liberty. Demand an open mind and fair hearing for every idea. Hold sacred the right of expression: protect the freedom of speech and press. Suffer not Thought to be forcibly limited and opinions proscribed. Make conscience free, undisciplined. Allow no curtailment of aspirations and ideals. These are the levers of progress, the fountain-head of joy and beauty.

Join your efforts, lovers of humanity. Do not uphold the hand that strangles Life. Align yourselves with the dreamers of the Better Day. The cause is worthy, the need urgent. The future looks towards you, its voice calls you, calls.

May it not call in vain.

And you, fellow workers in factory, mine, and field, a great mission is yours. You, the feeders of the world and the creators of its wealth, you are the most interested in the fate of your country. The menace of despotism is greatest to you. Long has your masters' service humiliated and degraded you. Will you permit yourselves to be driven into still more abject slavery? Your emancipation is your work. Others may help, but you alone can win. In shop and union, take up this your greatest problem. Let not the least of you be victimized. Remember, an injury to one is the concern of all. No worker can stand alone in the face of organized capitalism with all its legislative and military weapons. Learn solidarity: each with a common purpose, all with a common effort. Know your enemy: there is no "mutual interest" between the robber and the robbed. Understand your true friends. You'll always find them maligned and persecuted by your enemies. The idealists, the seekers of the slaveless world, speak from your heart. Give them hearing.

Your fate, the fate of the country, is in your hands. Yours is the mightiest power. There is no strength in the Government, except you give it. No strength in your masters, except you suffer it. The only true mastery is in you, the working class, in your power to feed and clothe the world and make it joyous. The greatest power, for good or evil. Use it for liberty, for justice. Allow no suppression of the freedom of thought and speech, for it is a snare for your undoing. Sooner or later every suppression comes home to labor, for its greater enslavement. Realize the menace of deportation, of the principle of banishment and exile. 'Tis the latest method of the American plutocracy to silence the discontent of the workers. Lose no time. It is of the most vital importance to you. It threatens you, your union, your very existence. Take the matter up in your organizations. The fortunes of labor in America are at stake. Only your united effort can conquer the peril that menaces you. Take action. Rouse the workers of the whole country. In union and solidarity, in clear purpose and courage is your only salvation.

Quotations from American and Foreign Authors Which Would Fall Under the Criminal Anarchy Law, Espionage Law, Etc.

These authors, distinguished thinkers, philosophers and humanitarians of world-wide renown would, if still alive and of foreign birth, not be permitted on American shores if they tried to land here, or, if born Americans, they would be threatened by deportation to the Island of Guam.

Abraham Lincoln

The man who will not investigate both sides of a question is dishonest.

The cause of civil liberty must not be surrendered at the end of one or even one hundred defeats.

The authors of the Declaration of Independence meant it to be a stumbling block to those who in after times might seek to turn free people back into the paths of despotism.

I have always thought that all men should be free, but if any should be slaves, it should be first those who desire it for themselves, and secondly those who desire it for others.

If there is anything that it is the duty of the whole people never to entrust to any hands but their own, that thing is the preservation and perpetuity of their own liberties.

Thomas Jefferson

All eyes are opening to the right of man. The general spread of the light of science has already laid open to every view the palpable truth, that the mass of mankind has not been born with saddles on their backs, nor a favored few booted and spurred, ready to ride them legitimately, by the grace of God.

Societies exist under three forms, sufficiently distinguishable: (1) Without government, as among our Indians. (2) Under governments wherein the will of everyone has a just influence; as is the case in England, in a slight degree, and in our States, in a great one. (3) Under governments of force; as is the case in all other monarchies, and in most of the other republics. To have an idea of the curse of existence under these last, they must be seen. It is a government of wolves over sheep. It is a problem, not clear in my mind, that the first condition is not the best. But I believe it to be inconsistent with any great degree of population. The second state has a great deal of good in it. The mass of mankind under that, enjoys a precious degree of liberty and happiness. It has its evils, too; the principal of which is the turbulence to which it is subject. But weight this against the oppressions of monarchy, and it becomes nothing. Even this evil is productive of good. It prevents the degeneracy of governments, and nourishes a general attention to the public affairs. I hold it, that a little rebellion, now and then, is a good thing, and as necessary in the political world as storms in the physical. Unsuccessful rebellions, indeed, generally establish the encroachments on the rights of the people which have produced them. An observation of this truth should render honest republican governors so mild in their punishment of rebellions, as not to discourage them too much. It is a medicine necessary for the sound health of governments.

We have long enough suffered under the base prostitution of law to party passions in one judge, and the imbecility of another.

It is error alone which needs the support of government. Truth can stand by itself.

William Lloyd Garrison

Liberty for each, for all, and forever.

No person will rule over me with my consent. I will rule over no man.

Enslave the liberty of but one human being and the liberties of the world are put in peril.

When I look at these crowded thousands, and see them trample on their consciences and the rights of their fellowmen at the bidding of a piece of parchment, I say, my curse be on the Constitution of the United States.

Why, sir, no freedom of speech or inquiry is conceded to me in this land. Am I not vehemently told both at the North and the South that I have no right to meddle with the question of slavery? And my right to speak on any other subject, in opposition to public opinion, is equally denied to me.

I am aware that many object to the severity of my language; but is there not cause for severity? I will be as harsh as Truth, and as uncompromising as Justice. On this subject I do not wish to think, or speak, or write, with moderation. No! No! Tell a man whose house is on fire to give a moderate alarm; tell him to moderately rescue his wife from the hands of the ravisher; tell the mother to gradually extricate her babe from the fire into which it has fallen—but urge me not to use moderation in a cause like the present. I am in earnest—I will not equivocate I will not excuse I will not retreat a single inch—and I will be heard. The apathy of the people is enough to make every statue leap from its pedestal and hasten to the resurrection of the dead. —In the first issue of the *Liberator*, January 1, 1831.

Wendell Phillips

If there is anything that cannot bear free thought, let it crack.

Nothing but Freedom, Justice, and Truth is of any permanent advantage to the mass of mankind. To these society, left to itself, is always tending.

"The right to think, to know and to utter," as John Milton said, is the dearest of all liberties. Without this right, there can be no liberty to any people; with it, there can be no slavery.

When you have convinced thinking men that it is right, and humane men that it is just, you will gain your cause. Men always lose half of what is gained by violence. What is gained by argument, is gained forever.

The manna of liberty must be gathered each day, or it is rotten.

Only by unintermitted agitation can a people be kept sufficiently awake to principle not to let liberty be smothered in material prosperity.

Let us believe that the whole truth can never do harm to the whole of virtue; and remember that in order to get the whole of truth, you must allow every man, right or wrong, freely to utter his conscience, and protect him in so doing. Entire unshackled freedom for every man's life, no matter how wide its range. The community which dares not protect its humblest and most hated member in the free utterance of his opinions, no matter how false or hateful, is only a gang of slaves.

Stephen Pearl Andrews

Governments have hitherto been established, and have apologized for the unseemly fact of their existence, from the necessity of establishing and maintaining order; but order has never yet been maintained, revolutions and violent outbreaks have never yet been ended, public peace and harmony have never yet been secured, for the precise reason that the organic, essential, and indestructible natures of the objects which it was attempted to reduce to order have always been constricted and infringed by every such attempt. Just in proportion as the effort is less and less made to reduce men to order, just in that proportion they become more orderly, as witness the difference in the state of society in Austria and the United States. Plant an army of one hundred thousand soldiers in New York, as at Paris, to preserve the peace, and we should have a bloody revolution in a week; and be assured that the only remedy for what little of turbulence remains among us, as compared with European societies, will be found to be more liberty. When there remain positively no external restrictions, there will be positively no disturbance, provided always certain regulating principles of justice, to which I shall advert presently, are accepted and enter into the public mind, serving as substitutes for every species of repressive laws.

Henry George

In our time, as in times before, creep on the insidious forces that, producing inequality, destroy Liberty. On the horizon the clouds begin to lower. Liberty calls to us again. We must follow her further; we must trust her fully. Either we must wholly accept her or she will not stay. It is not enough that men should vote; it is not enough that they should be theoretically equal before the law. They must have liberty to avail themselves of the opportunities and means of life; they must stand on equal terms with reference to the bounty of nature. Either this, or Liberty withdraws her light! Either this, or darkness comes on, and the very forces that progress has evolved turn to powers that work destruction. This is the universal law. This is the lesson of the centuries. Unless its foundations be laid in justice the social structure cannot stand.

Henry David Thoreau

Law never made men a whit more just; and, by means of their respect for it, even the well-disposed are daily made the agents of injustice. A common and natural result of an undue respect for law is that you may see a file of soldiers, colonel, captain, corporal, privates, powder-monkeys, and all, marching in admirable order over hill and dale to the wars, against their wills, aye, against their common sense and consciences, which makes it very steep marching indeed, and produces a palpitation of the heart. They have no doubt that it is a damnable business in which they are concerned; they are all peaceably inclined. Now, what are they? Men at all? Or small movable forts and magazines, at the service of some unscrupulous man in power?

The mass of men serve the State thus, not as men mainly, but as machines, with their bodies. They are the standing army, and the militia, jailers, constables, posse comitatus, etc. In most cases there is no free exercise whatever of the judgment or of the moral sense; but they put themselves on a level with wood and earth and stones; and wooden men can perhaps be manufactured that will serve the purpose as well. Such command no more respect than men of straw or a lump of dirt. They have the same sort of worth only as horses and dogs. Yet such as these even are commonly esteemed good citizens.

Others—as most legislators, politicians, lawyers, ministers, and office-holders—serve the State chiefly with their heads; and as they rarely make any moral distinctions, they are as likely to serve the devil, without intending it, as God.

How does it become a man to behave toward this American government today? I answer, that he cannot without disgrace, be associated with it. I cannot for an instant recognize that political organization as my government which is the slave's government also.

All men recognize the right of revolution; that is, the right to refuse allegiance to, and to resist, the government, when its tyranny or its inefficiency are great and unendurable.

Ralph Waldo Emerson

It will never make any difference to a hero what the laws are.

For what avail the plough or sail

Or land or life, if freedom fail?

The wise know that foolish legislation is a rope of sand which perishes in the twisting.

Our distrust is very expensive. The money we spend for courts and prisons is very ill laid out.

Every actual State is corrupt. Good men must not obey the laws too well. What satire on government can equal the severity of censure conveyed in the word politics which now for ages has signified cunning, intimating that the State is a trick?

No law can be sacred to me but that of my nature. Good and bad are but names very readily transferable to that or this; the only right is what is after my constitution, the only wrong what is against it. A man is to carry himself in the presence of all opposition, as if everything were titular and ephemeral but him. I am ashamed to think how easily we capitulate to badges and names, to large societies and dead institutions.

Edmund Burke

All writers on the science of policy are agreed, and they agree with experience, that all governments must frequently infringe the rules of justice to support themselves; that truth must give way to dissimulation, honesty to convenience, and humanity to the reigning interest. The whole of this mystery of iniquity is called the reason of state. It is a reason which I own I cannot penetrate. What sort of a protection is this of the general right, that is maintained by infringing the rights of particulars? What sort of justice is this which is enforced by breaches of its own laws? These paradoxes I leave to be solved by the able heads of legislators and politicians. For my part, I say what a plain man would say on such occasion. I can never believe that any institution, agreeable to nature, and proper for mankind, could find it necessary, or even expedient, in any case whatsoever, to do what the best and worthiest instinct of mankind warn us to avoid. But no wonder that what is set up in opposition to the state of nature should preserve itself by trampling upon the law of nature.

Thomas Paine

To argue with a man who has renounced his reason is like giving medicine to the dead.

The more perfect civilization is, the less occasion has it for government because the more does it regulate its own affairs, and govern itself; but so contrary is the practice of old governments to the reason of the case, that the expenses of them increase in the proportion they ought to diminish. It is but few general laws that civilized life requires, and those of such common usefulness, that, whether they are enforced by the forms of government or not, the effect will be nearly the same. If we consider what the principles are that first condense man into society, and what the motives that regulate their mutual intercourse afterwards, we shall find, by the time we arrive at what is called government, that nearly the whole of the business is performed by the natural operation of the parts upon each other.

Society in every state is a blessing, but government, even in its best state, is but a necessary evil; in its worst state, an intolerable one.

The trade of governing has always been monopolized by the most ignorant and the most rascally individuals of mankind.

John Stuart Mill

Mankind can hardly be too often reminded, that there was once a man named Socrates, between whom and the legal authorities and public opinion of his time, there took place a memorable collision. Born in an age and country abounding in individual greatness, this man has been handed down to us by those who best knew both him and the age, as the most virtuous man in it; while we know him as the head and prototype of all subsequent teachers of virtue, the source equally of the lofty inspiration of Plato and the judicious utilitarianism of Aristotle, the two headsprings of ethical as of all other philosophy. Their acknowledged master of all the eminent thinkers who have since lived—whose fame, still growing after more than two thousand years, all but outweighs the whole remainder of the names which make his native city illustrious—was put to death by his countrymen, after a judicial conviction, for impiety and immorality. Impiety, in denying the Gods recognized by the State; indeed his accusers asserted (see the "Apologia") that he believed in no gods at all. Immorality, in being, by his doctrines and instructions, a "corrupter of youth." Of these charges the tribunal, there is every ground for believing, honestly found him guilty, and condemned the man who probably of all then born had deserved best of mankind, to be put to death as a criminal.

Herbert Spencer

When we have made our constitution purely democratic, thinks to himself the earnest reformer, we shall have brought government into harmony with absolute justice. Such a faith, though perhaps needful for the age, is a very erroneous one. By no process can coercion be made equitable. The freest form of government is only the least objectionable form. The rule of the many by the few we call tyranny: the rule of the few by the many is tyranny also, only of a less intense kind. "You shall do as we will, and not as you will," is in either case the declaration; and, if the hundred make it to ninety-nine instead of the ninety-nine to the hundred, it is only a fraction less immoral. Of two such parties, whichever fulfills this declaration, necessarily breaks the law of equal freedom: the only difference being that by the one it is broken in the persons of ninety-nine, whilst by the other it is broken in the persons of a hundred. And the merit of the democratic form of government consists solely in this—that it trespasses against the smallest number.

The very existence of majorities and minorities is indicative of an immoral state. The man whose character harmonizes with the moral law, we found to be one who can obtain complete happiness without establishing the happiness of his fellows. But the enactment of public arrangements by vote implies a society consisting of men otherwise constituted—implies that the desires of some cannot be satisfied without sacrificing the desires of others-implies that in the pursuit of their happiness the majority inflict a certain amount of unhappiness on the minority—implies, therefore, organic immorality. Thus, from another point of view, we again perceive that even in its most equitable form it is impossible for government to disassociate itself from evil; and further, that, unless the right to ignore the State is recognized, its acts must he essentially criminal.

Leo Tolstoy

The cause of the miserable condition of the workers is slavery. The cause of slavery is legislation. Legislation rests on organized violence. It follows that an improvement in the condition of the people is possible only through the abolition of organized violence. "But organized violence is government, and how can we live without governments? Without governments there will be chaos, anarchy; all the achievements of civilization will perish, and the people will revert to their primitive barbarism." But why should we suppose this? Why think that non-official people could not arrange it, not for themselves, but for others? We see, on the contrary, that in the most diverse matters people in our times arrange their own lives incomparably better than those who govern them arrange for them. Without the least help from government, and often in spite of the interference of government, people organize all sorts of social undertakings—workmen's unions, co-operative societies, railway companies, and syndicates. If collections for public works are needed, why should we suppose that free people could not without violence voluntarily collect the necessary means, and carry out all that is carried out by means of taxes, if only the undertakings in question are really useful for anybody? Why suppose that there cannot be tribunals without violence?

The robber generally plundered the rich, the governments generally plunder the poor and protect those rich who assist in their crimes. The robber doing his work risked his life, while the governments risk nothing, but base their whole activity on lies and deception. The robber did not compel anyone to join his band, the governments generally enroll their soldiers by force. All who paid the tax to the robber had equal security from danger. But in the state, the more anyone takes part in the organized fraud the more he receives not merely of protection, but also of reward.

The Russian Revolution and the Communist Party

1922

Preface

Clarity of ideas is not characteristic of the average mind. Many people still continue to think and to talk of the Russian Revolution and of the Bolsheviks as if the two were identical. In other words, as if nothing had happened in Russia during the last three years.

The great need of the present is to make clear the difference between that grand social event and the ruling political party—a difference as fundamental as it has been fatal to the Revolution.

The following pages present a clear and historically true picture of the ideals that inspired the Revolution, and of the role played by the Bolsheviks. This pamphlet conclusively proves what the Russian Revolution *is* and what the Bolshevik State, alias the Communist Party, *is not*.

I consider this brochure a very able, and for popular reading sufficiently exhaustive, analysis of the Russian Revolution and of the causes of its undoing. It may be regarded as an authoritative expression of the Anarchist movement of Russia, for it was written by Anarchists of different schools, some of them participants and all of them well versed in the events of the Revolution. It is the joint work of four well known Moscow Anarchists. Their names cannot be mentioned at present, in view of the fact that some of them are still in Russia. Nor are their names important in this connection: rather is it the subject and its treatment. I hereby accept full responsibility for the contents of the following pages, as I am also responsible for the rendering of the Russian manuscript into English.

July, 1922.

Alexander Berkman

The Russian Revolution And The Communist Party

The October Revolution was not the legitimate offspring of traditional Marxism. Russia but little resembled a country in which, according to Marx, "the concentration of the means of production and the socialization of the tools of labor reached the point where they can no longer be contained within their capitalistic shell. The shell bursts. ..."

In Russia, "the shell" burst unexpectedly. It burst at a stage of low technical and industrial development, when centralization of the means of production had made little progress. Russia was a country with a badly organized system of transportation, with a weak bourgeoisie and weak proletariat, but with a numerically strong and socially important peasant population. In short, it was a country in which, apparently, there could be no talk of irreconcilable antagonism between the grown industrial labor forces and a fully ripened capitalist system.

But the combination of circumstances in 1917 involved, particularly for Russia, an exceptional state of affairs which resulted in the catastrophic breakdown of her whole industrial system. "It was easy for Russia", Lenin justly wrote at the time, "to begin the socialist revolution in the peculiarly unique situation of 1917."

The specially favorable conditions for the beginning of the socialist revolution were:

1) the possibility of blending the slogans of the Social Revolution with the popular demand for the termination of the imperialistic

world war, which had produced great exhaustion and dissatisfaction among the masses;

2) the possibility of remaining, at least for a certain period after quitting the war, outside the sphere of influence of the capitalistic European groups that continued the world war;

3) the opportunity to begin, even during the short time of this respite, the work of internal organization and to prepare the foundation for revolutionary reconstruction;

4) the exceptionally favorable position of Russia, in case of possible new aggression on the part of West European imperialism, due to her vast territory and insufficient means of communication;

5) the advantages of such a condition in the event of civil war; and

6) the possibility of almost immediately satisfying the fundamental demands of the revolutionary peasantry, notwithstanding the fact that the essentially democratic viewpoint of the agricultural population was entirely different from the socialist program of the "party of the proletariat" which seized the reins of government.

Moreover, revolutionary Russia already had the benefit of a great experience — the experience of 1905, when the Tsarist autocracy succeeded in crushing the revolution for the very reason that the latter strove to be exclusively political and therefore could neither arouse the peasants nor inspire even a considerable part of the proletariat.

The World War, by exposing the complete bankruptcy of constitutional government, served to prepare and quicken the greatest movement of the people — a movement which, by virtue of its very essence, could develop only into a social revolution.

Anticipating the measures of the revolutionary government, often even in defiance of the latter, the revolutionary masses by their own initiative began, long before the October days, to put in practice their Social ideals. They took possession of the land, the factories, mines, mills, and the tools of production. They got rid of the more hated and dangerous representatives of government and authority. In their grand revolutionary outburst they destroyed every form of political and economic oppression. In the deeps of Russia the Social

Revolution was raging, when the October change took place in the capitals of Petrograd and Moscow.

The Communist Party, which was aiming at the dictatorship, from the very beginning correctly judged the situation. Throwing overboard the democratic planks of its platform, it energetically proclaimed the slogans of the Social Revolution, in order to gain control of the movement of the masses. In the course of the development of the Revolution, the Bolsheviks gave concrete form to certain fundamental principles and methods of Anarchist Communism, as for instance: the negation of parliamentarism, expropriation of the bourgeoisie, tactics of direct action, seizure of the means of production, establishment of the system of Workers' and Peasants' Councils (Soviets), and so forth.

Furthermore, the Communist Party exploited all the popular demands of the hour: termination of the war, all power to the revolutionary proletariat, the land for the peasants, etc. This, as we shall see later, base demagoguery proved of tremendous psychological effect in hastening and intensifying the revolutionary process.

But if it was easy, as Lenin said, to begin the Revolution, its further development and strengthening were to take place amid difficult surroundings.

The external position of Russia, as characterized by Lenin about the middle of 1918, continued to be "unusually complicated and dangerous", and "tempting for the neighboring imperialist States by its temporary weakness". The Socialist Soviet Republic was in an "extraordinarily unstable, very critical international position".

And, indeed, the whole subsequent external history of Russia is full of difficulties in consequence of the necessity of fighting ceaselessly, often on several fronts at once, against the agents of world imperialism, and even against common adventurers. Only after the final defeat of the Wrangel forces was at last put an end to direct armed interference in the affairs of Russia.

No less difficult and complex, even chaotic, was the internal situation of the country.

Complete breakdown of the whole industrial fabric; failure of the national economy; disorganization of the transportation system, hunger, unemployment; relative lack of organization among the workers; unusually complex and contradictory conditions of peasant life; the psychology of the "'petty proprietor", inimical to the new Soviet regime; sabotage of Soviet work by the technical intelligentsia; the great lack in the Party of trained workers familiar with local conditions, and the practical inefficiency of the Party heads; finally, according to the frank admission of the acknowledged leader of the Bolsheviks, "the greatest hatred, by the masses, and distrust of everything governmental" — that was the situation in which the first and most difficult steps of the Revolution had to be made.

It must also be mentioned that there were still other specific problems with which the revolutionary government had to deal. Namely, the deep-seated contradictions and even antagonisms between the interests and aspirations of the various social groups of the country. The most important of these were:

(a) the most advanced, and in industrial centers the most influential, group of factory proletarians. Notwithstanding their relative cultural and technical backwardness, these elements favored the application of true communist methods;

(b) the numerically powerful peasant population, whose economic attitude was decisive, particularly at a time of industrial prostration and blockade. This class looked with distrust and even hatred upon all attempts of the Communist government to play the guardian and control their economic activities;

(c) the very large and psychologically influential group (in the sense of forming public opinion, even if of a panicky character) of the common citizenry: the residue of the upper bourgeoisie, technical specialists, small dealers, petty bosses, commercial agents of every kind—a numerous group, in which were also to be found functionaries of the old regime who adapted themselves and were serving the Soviet government, now and then sabotaging; elements tempted by the opportunities of the new order of things and seeking to make a career; and, finally, persons torn out of their habitual modes of life and literally starving. This class was approximately estimated at 70% of the employees of Soviet institutions.

Naturally, each of these groups looked upon the Revolution with their own eyes, judged its further possibilities from their own point of view, and in their own peculiar manner reacted on the measures of the revolutionary government.

All these antagonisms rending the country and, frequently clashing in bloody strife, inevitably tended to nourish counter-revolution—not mere conspiracy or rebellion, but the terrific convulsion of a country experiencing two world cataclysms at once: war and social revolution.

Thus the political party that assumed the role of dictator was faced by problems of unprecedented difficulty. The Communist Party did not shrink from their solution, and in that is its immortal historic merit.

Notwithstanding the many deep antagonisms, in spite of the apparent absence of the conditions necessary for a social revolution, it was too late to discuss about driving back the uninvited guest, and await a new, more favorable opportunity. Only blind, dogmatic or positively reactionary elements could imagine that the Revolution could have been "made differently". The Revolution was not and could not be a mechanical product of the abstract human will. It was an organic process burst with elemental force from the very needs of the people, from the complex combination of circumstances that determined their existence.

To return to tile old political and economic regime, that of industrial feudalism, was out of the question. It was impossible, and first of all because it were the denial of the greatest conquest of the Revolution: the right of every worker to a decent human life. It was also impossible because of the fundamental principles of the new national economy: the old regime was inherently inimical to the development of free social relationship—it had no room for labor initiative.

It was apparent that the only right and wholesome solution—which could save the Revolution from its external enemies, free it from the inner strife which rent the country, broaden and deepen the Revolution itself—lay in the direct, creative initiative of the toiling masses. Only they who had for centuries borne the heaviest burdens could through conscious systematic effort find the road to a new, regenerated society. And that was to be the fitting culmination of their unexampled revolutionary zeal.

Lenin himself, replying in one of his works to the question, "How is the discipline of the revolutionary party of the proletariat to be maintained, how to be strengthened?" clearly and definitely replied:

"By knowing how to meet, to combine, to some extent even to merge, if you will, with the broad masses of the toilers, mainly with the proletariat, but also with the non-proletarian laboring masses".

However, this thought was and still remains, on the whole, in irreconcilable conflict, with the spirit of Marxism in its official Bolshevik interpretation, and particularly with Lenin's authoritative view of it.

For years trained in their peculiar "underground" social philosophy, in which fervent faith in the Social Revolution was in some odd manner blended with their no less fanatical faith in State centralization, the Bolsheviks devised an entirely new science of tactics. It is to the effect that the preparation and consummation of the Social Revolution necessitates the organization of a special conspirative staff, consisting exclusively of the theoreticians of the movement, vested with dictatorial powers for the purpose of clarifying and perfecting beforehand, by their own conspirative means, the class-consciousness of the proletariat.

Thus the fundamental characteristic of Bolshevik psychology was distrust of the masses, of the proletariat. Left to themselves, the masses — according to Bolshevik conviction — could rise only to the consciousness of the petty reformer.

The road that leads to the direct creativeness of the masses was thus forsaken.

According to Bolshevik conception, the masses are "dark", mentally crippled by ages of slavery. They are multi-colored: besides the revolutionary advance-guard they comprise great numbers of the indifferent and many self-seekers. The masses, according to the old but still correct maxim of Rousseau, must be made free by force. To educate them to liberty one must not hesitate to use compulsion and violence.

"Proletarian compulsion in all its forms", writes Bukharin, one of the foremost Communist theoreticians, "beginning with summary execution and ending with compulsory labor is, however paradoxical it may sound, a method of reworking the human material of the capitalistic epoch into Communist humanity".

This cynical doctrinairism, this fanatical quasi-philosophy flavored with Communist pedagogic sauce and aided by the pressure of "canonized officials" (expression of the prominent Communist and labor leader Shliapnikov) represent the actual methods of the Party dictatorship, which retains the trademark of the "dictatorship of the proletariat" merely for gala affairs at home and for advertisement abroad. Already in the first days of the Revolution, early in 1918, when Lenin first announced to the world his socio-economic program in its minutest details, the roles of the people and of the Party in the revolutionary reconstruction were strictly separated and definitely assigned. On the one hand, an absolutely submissive socialist herd, a dumb people; on the other, the omniscient, all-controlling Political Party. What is inscrutable to all, is an open book to It. In the land there may be only one indisputable source of truth—the State. But the Communist State is, in essence and practice, the dictatorship of the Party only, or—more correctly—the dictatorship of its Central Committee. Each and every citizen must be, first and foremost, the servant of the State, its obedient functionary, unquestioningly executing the will of his master—if not as a matter of conscience, then out of fear. All free initiative, of the individual as well as of the collectivity, is eliminated from the vision of the State. The people's Soviets are transformed into sections of the Ruling Party; the Soviet institutions become soulless offices, mere transmitters of the will of the center to the periphery. All expressions of State activity must be stamped with the approving seal of Communism as interpreted by the faction in power. Everything else is considered superfluous, useless and dangerous.

This system of barrack absolutism, supported by bullet and bayonet, has subjugated every phase of life, stopping neither before the destruction of the best cultural values, nor before the most stupendous squandering of human life and energy.

By its declaration *L'état c'est moi*, the Bolshevik dictatorship has assumed entire responsibility for the Revolution in all its historic and ethical implications

Having paralyzed the constructive efforts of the people, the Communist Party could henceforth count only on its own initiative. By what means, then, did the Bolshevik dictatorship expect to use to best advantage the resources of the Social Revolution? What road did it choose, not merely to subject the masses mechanically to its authority, but also to educate them, to inspire them with advanced socialist ideas, and to stimulate them—exhausted as they were by long war, economic ruin and police rule—with new faith in socialist reconstruction? What has it substituted in place of the revolutionary enthusiasm which burned so intensely before?

Two things, which comprised the beginning and the end of the constructive activities of the Bolshevik dictatorship: 1) the theory of the Communist State, and 2) terrorism.

In his speeches about the Communist program, in discussions at conferences and congresses, and in his celebrated pamphlet on "Infantile Sickness of 'Leftism' in Communism", Lenin gradually shaped that peculiar doctrine of the Communist State which was fated to play the dominant role in the attitude of the Party and to determine all the subsequent steps of the Bolsheviks in the sphere of practical politics. It is the doctrine of a zigzag political road: of "respites" and "tributes", agreements and compromises, profitable retreats, advantageous withdrawals and surrenders—a truly classical theory of compromise.

Scorning the "chuckling and giggling of the lackeys of the bourgeoisie", Lenin calls upon the laboring masses to "steer down the wind", to retreat, to wait and watch, to go slowly, and so on. Not the fiery spirit of Communism, but sober commercialism which can successfully bargain for a few crumbs of socialism from the still unconquered bourgeoisie—that is the "need of the hour". To encourage and develop the virtues of the trader, the spirit of parsimony and profitable dealing: that is the first commandment to the "regenerated" people.

In the pamphlet referred to, Lenin scouts all stereotyped morality and compares the tactics of his Party with those of a military commander, ignoring the gulf which divides them and their aims. All means are good that lead to victory. There are compromises and compromises. "The whole history of Bolshevism before and after the October Revolution", Lenin sermonizes the "naive German left Communists" who are stifling in their own revolutionary fervor, "is replete with instances of agreements and compromises with other parties, the bourgeoisie included". To prove his assertion, Lenin enumerates in great detail various cases of bargaining with bourgeoisie parties, beginning with 1905 and up to the adoption by the Bolsheviks, at the time of the October Revolution, "of the agrarian platform of the socialists-revolutionists, in toto, without change".

Compromise and bargaining, for which the Bolsheviks so unmercifully and justly denounced and stigmatized all the other factions of State Socialism, now become the Bethlehem Star pointing the way to revolutionary reconstruction. Naturally, such methods could not fail to lead, with fatal inevitability, into the swamp of conformation, hypocrisy and unprincipledness.

The Brest-Litovsk peace; the agrarian policy with its spasmodic changes from the poorest class of peasantry to the peasant exploiter; the perplexed, panicky attitude to the labor unions; the fitful Policy in regard to technical experts, with its theoretical and practical swaying from collegiate management of industries to "one-man power"; nervous appeals to West European capitalism, over the heads of the home and foreign proletariat; filially, the latest inconsistent and zigzaggy, but incontrovertible and assured restoration of the abolished bourgeoisie—such is the new system of Bolshevism. A system of unprecedented shamelessness practiced on a monster scale, a policy of outrageous double-dealing in which the left hand of the Communist Party is beginning consciously to ignore, and even to deny, on principle, what its right hand is doing; when, for instance, it is proclaimed, on the one hand, that the most important problem of the moment is the struggle against the small bourgeoisie (and, incidentally, in stereotyped Bolshevik phraseology, against anarchist elements), while on the other hand are issued new decrees creating the techno-economic and psychological conditions necessary for the restoration and strengthening of that same bourgeoisie—that is the Bolshevik policy which will forever stand as a monument of the thoroughly false, thoroughly contradictory, concerned only in self-preservation, opportunistic policy of the Communist Party dictatorship.

However loud that dictatorship may shout about the great success of its new political methods, it remains the most tragic fact that the worst and most incurable wounds of the Revolution were received at the hands of the Communist dictatorship itself.

An inevitable consequence of Communist Party rule was also the other "method" of Bolshevik management: terrorism.

Long ago Engels said that the proletariat does not need the State to protect liberty, but needs it for the purpose of crushing its opponents; and that when it will be possible to speak of liberty, there will be no government. The Bolsheviks adopted this maxim not only as their socio-political axiom during the "transition period", but gave it universal application.

Terrorism always was and still remains the *ultima ratio* of government alarmed for its existence. Terrorism is tempting with its tremendous possibilities. It offers a mechanical solution, as it were, in hopeless situations. Psychologically it is explained as a matter of self-defense, as the necessity of throwing off responsibility the better to strike the enemy.

But the principles of terrorism unavoidably rebound to the fatal injury of liberty and revolution. Absolute power corrupts and defeats its partisans no less than its opponents. A people that knows not liberty becomes accustomed to dictatorship: fighting despotism and counter-revolution, terrorism itself becomes their efficient school.

Once on the road of terrorism, the State necessarily becomes estranged from the people. It must reduce to the possible minimum the circle of persons vested with extraordinary powers, in the name of the safety of the State. And then is born what may be called the panic of authority. The dictator, the despot, is always cowardly. He suspects treason everywhere. And the more terrified he becomes, the wilder rages his frightened imagination, incapable of distinguishing real danger from fancied. He sows broadcast discontent, antagonism, hatred. Having chosen this course, the State is doomed to follow it to the very end.

The Russian people remained silent, and in their name—in the guise of mortal combat with counter-revolution—the government initiated the most merciless warfare against all political opponents of the Communist Party. Every vestige of liberty was torn out by the roots. Freedom of thought, of the press, of public assembly, self-determination of the worker and of his unions, the freedom of labor—all were declared old rubbish, doctrinaire nonsense, "bourgeois prejudices", or intrigues of reviving counter-revolution. Science, art, education fell under suspicion. Science is to investigate and teach only the truths of the Communist State: the schools and universities are speedily transformed into Party schools.

Election campaigns, as for instance the recent re-elections to the Moscow Soviet (1921), involve the arrest and imprisonment of opposition candidates who are not favored by the authorities. With entire impunity the government exposes non-Communist candidates to public insult and derision on the pages of the official newspapers pasted on bulletin boards. By numberless stratagems the electors are cajoled and menaced, in turn, and the result of the so-called elections is the complete perversion of the people's will.

State terrorism is exercised through government organs known as Extraordinary Commissions. Vested with unlimited powers, independent of any control and practically irresponsible, possessing their own "simplified" forms of investigation and procedure, with a numerous staff of ignorant, corrupt and brutal agents, these Commissions have within a short time become not only the terror of actual or fancied counter-revolution, but also — and much more so — the most virulent ulcer on the revolutionary body of the country.

The all-pervading secret police methods, the inseparable from them system of provocation, the division of the population into well-meaning and ill-disposed, have gradually transformed the Struggle for the new world into an unbridled debauch of espionage, pillage and violence.

No reactionary régime ever dominated the life and liberty of its citizens with such arbitrariness and despotism as the alleged "dictatorship of the proletariat". As in the old days of Tsarism, the "*okhranka*" (secret police section) rules the land. The Soviet prisons are filled with socialists and revolutionists of every shade of political opinion. Physical violence toward political prisoners and hunger strikes in prison are again the order of the day. Summary executions, not only of individuals but en masse, are common occurrences. The Socialist State has not scrupled to resort to a measure which even the most brutal bourgeois governments did not dare to use: the system of hostages. Relationship or even casual friendship is sufficient ground for merciless persecution and, quite frequently, for capital punishment.

Gross and barbaric contempt for the most elementary human rights has become an axiom of the Communist Government.

With logical inevitability the Extraordinary Commissions have gradually grown into a monstrous autocratic mechanism, independent and unaccountable, with power over life and death. Appeal is impossible, non-existent. Even the supreme organs of State authority are powerless before the Extraordinary Commissions, as proven by bitter experience.

The Bolshevik Party is not in the habit of scorning any perversion of truth to stigmatize every anti-Bolshevik criticism or protest as "conspiracy" of one of the "right" socialist parties: of the social-democratic Mensheviks and Socialist-Revolutionists. Thus the Communists seek to justify brutal repressions against the "right elements". In regard to the Anarchists, however, Bolshevist terrorism cannot be "justified" by such means.

It is apropos here to sketch, though very briefly, the mutual relations between Anarchism and Bolshevism during the Revolution.

When, in the first days of the Revolution (1917), the laboring masses began the destruction of the system of private ownership and of government, the Anarchists worked shoulder to shoulder with them. The October Revolution instinctively followed the path marked out by the great popular outburst, naturally reflecting Anarchist tendencies. The Revolution destroyed the old State mechanism and proclaimed in political life the principle of the federation of soviets. It employed the method of direct expropriation to abolish private capitalistic ownership: the peasants and workers expropriated the landlords, chased the financiers from the banks, seized the factories, mines, mills and shops. In the field of economic reconstruction the Revolution established the principle of the federation of shop and factory committees for the management of production. House committees looked after the proper assignment of living quarters.

In this early phase of the October Revolution, the Anarchists aided the people with all the power at their command, and worked hand in hand with the Bolsheviks in supporting and strengthening the new principles. Among the legion of enthusiastic fighters of the Revolution, who to the end remained true to the ideals and methods of Anarchism, we may particularly mention here Justin Zhook, the founder of the famous Schluesselburg powder mill, who lost his life while performing revolutionary military duty; also Zhelesnyakov, who with rare strength and courage dispersed the Constituent Assembly, and who afterwards fell fighting against counter-revolutionary invasion.

But as soon as the Bolsheviks succeeded in gaining control of the movement of the masses, the work of social reconstruction suffered a sharp change in its character and forms.

From now on the Bolsheviks, under cover of the dictatorship of the proletariat, use every effort to build up a centralized bureaucratic State. All who interpreted the Social Revolution as, primarily, the self-determination of the masses, the introduction of free, non-governmental Communism—they are henceforth doomed to persecution. This persecution was directed, first of all, against the critics from "the left", the Anarchists. In April, 1918, the ruling Communist Party decided to abolish all Anarchist organizations. Without warning, on the night of April 12th, the Anarchist club of Moscow was surrounded by artillery and machine guns, and those present on the premises ordered to surrender. Fire was opened on those resisting. The Anarchist quarters were raided, and the following day the entire Anarchist press was suppressed.

Since then the persecution of Anarchists and of their organizations has assumed a systematic character. On the one hand our comrades were perishing on the military fronts, fighting counter- revolution; on the other, they were struck down by the Bolshevik State by means of the Extraordinary Commissions (*Tcheka*).

The further the ruling Party departed from the path marked out by the October Revolution, the more determinedly it oppressed the other revolutionary elements and particularly the Anarchists. In November, 1918, the All-Russian Conference of the Anarcho-Syndicalists, held in Moscow, was arrested *in corpore*. The other Anarchist organizations were broken up and terrorized. Because of the total impossibility of legal activity, some Anarchists decided to "go underground". Several of them, in cooperation with some left Socialist-Revolutionists, resorted to terrorism. On September 25, 1919, they exploded a bomb in the building (Leontevsky Pereulok) in which the Moscow Committee of the Party was in session. The Anarchist organizations of Moscow, not considering terrorism a solution of the difficulties, publicly expressed disapproval of the tactics of the underground group. The government, however, replied with repressions against all Anarchists. Many members of the underground group were executed, a number of Moscow Anarchists were arrested, and in the provinces every expression of the Anarchist movement was suppressed. The finding, during a search, of such Anarchist literature as the works of Kropotkin or Bakunin, led to arrest.

Only in the Ukraine, where the power of the Bolsheviks was comparatively weak, owing to the wide-spread rebel-peasant movement known as the *Makhnovstschina* (from its leader, the Anarchist Makhno), the Anarchist movement continued to some extent active. The advance of Wrangel into the heart of the Ukraine and the inability of the Red Army to halt his progress, caused Makhno temporarily to suspend his struggle with the Bolsheviks for free Soviets and the self-determination of the laboring masses. He offered his help to the Bolsheviks to fight the common enemy Wrangel. The offer was accepted, and a contract officially concluded between the Soviet Government and the army of Makhno.

Wrangel was defeated and his army dispersed, with Makhno playing no inconsiderable part in this great military triumph. But with the liquidation of Wrangel, Makhno became unnecessary and dangerous to the Bolsheviks. It was decided to get rid of him, to put an end to "*Makhnovstschina*", and, incidentally, dispose of the Anarchists at large. The Bolshevik government betrayed Makhno: the Red forces treacherously surrounded Makhno's army demanding surrender. At the same time all the delegates who had arrived in Kharkov to participate in the Anarchist Congress, for which official permission had been given, were arrested, as well as the Anarchists resident in Kharkov and the comrades still en route to the Congress.

Yet, in spite of all the provocative and terroristic tactics of the Bolsheviks against them, the Anarchists of Russia refrained, during the whole period of civil war, from protesting to the workers of Europe and America — aye, even to those of Russia itself — fearing that such action might be prejudicial to the interests of the Russian Revolution and that it may aid the common enemy, world imperialism.

But with the termination of civil war the position of the Anarchists grew even worse. The new policy of the Bolsheviks of open compromise with the bourgeois world became clearer, more definite, and ever sharper their break with the revolutionary aspirations of the working masses. The struggle against Anarchism, till then often masked by the excuse of fighting "banditism in the guise of Anarchism", now became open and frank warfare against Anarchist ideals and ideas, as such.

The Kronstadt events offered the Bolsheviks the desired pretext for completely "liquidating" the Anarchists. Wholesale arrests were instituted throughout Russia. Irrespective of factional adherence, practically all known Russian Anarchists were taken into the police net. To this day all of them remain in prison, without any charges having been preferred against them. In the night of April 25th-26th, 1921, all the political prisoners in the Bootirka prison (Moscow), to the number of over 400, consisting of representatives of the right and left wings of socialist parties and members of Anarchist organizations, were forcibly taken from the prison and transferred. On that occasion many of the prisoners suffered brutal violence: women were dragged down the steps by their hair, and a number of the politicals sustained serious injuries. The prisoners were divided into several groups and sent to various prisons in the provinces. Of their further fate we have so far been unable to receive definite information.

Thus did the Bolsheviks reply to the revolutionary enthusiasm and deep faith which inspired the masses in the beginning of their great struggle for liberty and justice—a reply that expressed itself in the policy of compromise abroad and terrorism at home.

This policy proved fatal: it corrupted and disintegrated the Revolution, poisoned it, stayed its soul, destroyed its moral, spiritual significance. By its despotism; by stubborn, petty paternalism; by the perfidy which replaced its former revolutionary idealism; by its stifling formalism and criminal indifference to the interests and aspirations of the masses; by its cowardly suspicion and distrust of the people at large, the "dictatorship of the proletariat" hopelessly cut itself off from the laboring masses.

Thrust back from direct participation in the constructive work of the Revolution, harassed at every step, the victim of constant supervision and control by the Party, the proletariat is becoming accustomed to consider the Revolution and its further fortunes as the private, personal affair of the Bolsheviks. In vain does the Communist Party seek by ever new decrees to preserve its hold upon the country's life. The people have seen through the rear meaning of the Party dictatorship. They know its narrow, selfish dogmatism, its cowardly opportunism; they are aware of its internal decay, its intrigues behind the scenes.

In the land where, after three years of tremendous effort, of terrible and heroic sacrifice, there should have come to bloom the wonder-flower of Communism—alas, even its withered buds are killed in distrust, apathy, and enmity.

Thus came about the era of revolutionary stagnation, of sterility, which cannot be cured by any political party methods, and which demonstrates the complete social atrophy.

The swamp of compromise into which Bolshevik dictatorship had sunk proved fatal to the Revolution: it became poisoned by its noxious miasma. In vain do the Bolsheviks point to the imperialistic world war as the cause of Russia's economic breakdown; in vain do they ascribe it to the blockade and the attacks of armed counter-revolution. Not in them is the real source of the collapse and debacle.

No blockade, no wars with foreign reaction could dismay or conquer the revolutionary people whose unexampled heroism, self-sacrifice and perseverance defeated all its external enemies. On the contrary, it is probable that civil war really helped the Bolsheviks. It served to keep alive popular enthusiasm and nurtured the hope that, with the end of war, the ruling Communist Party will make effective the new revolutionary principles and secure the people in the enjoyment of the fruits of the Revolution. The masses looked forward to the yearned-for opportunity for social and economic liberty. Paradoxical as it may sound, the Communist dictatorship had no better ally, in the sense of strengthening and prolonging its life, than the reactionary forces which fought against it.

It was only the termination of the wars which permitted a full view of the economic and psychological demoralization to which the blindly despotic policy of the dictatorship brought the revolutionary country. Then it became evident that the most formidable danger to the Revolution was not outside, but within the country: a danger resulting from the very nature of the social and economic arrangements which characterize the present "transitory stage".

We fully realize the gross error of the theoreticians of bourgeois political economy who wilfully ignore the study of [historical] evolution from the historical-social viewpoint, and stupidly confound the system of State capitalism with that of the socialist dictatorship. The Bolsheviks are quite right when they insist that the two types of socio-economic development are "diametrically opposed in their essential character." However, it was wrong and useless to pretend that such a form of industrial life as expressed in the present system of proletarian dictatorship is anything essentially different from State capitalism.

As a matter of fact, the proletarian dictatorship, as it actually exists, is in no sense different from State capitalism.

The distinctive characteristics of the latter—inherent social antagonisms—are abolished only formally in the Soviet Republic. In reality those antagonisms exist and arc very deep-seated The exploitation of labor, the enslavement of the worker and peasant, the cancellation of the citizen as a human being, as a personality, and his transformation into a microscopic part of the universal economic mechanism owned by the government; the creation of privileged groups favored by the State; the system of compulsory labor service and its punitive organs—such are the characteristic features of State capitalism.

All these features are also to be found in the present Russian system. It were unpardonable naivety, or still more unpardonable hypocrisy, to pretend—as do Bolshevik theoreticians, especially Bukharin—that universal compulsory labor service in the system of the proletarian dictatorship is, in contradistinction to State capitalism, "the self-organization of the masses for purposes of labor", or that the existing "mobilization of industry is the strengthening of socialism", and that "State Coercion in the system of proletarian dictatorship is a means of building the Communist society".

A year ago Trotsky, at the Tenth Congress of the Communist Party of Russia, thundered against the "bourgeois notion" that compulsory labor is not productive. He sought to convince his audience that the main problem is to "draw the worker into the process of labor, not by external methods of coercion, but by means internal, psychological". But when he approached the concrete application of this principle, he advocated a "very complex system, involving methods of an ethical nature, as well as premiums and punishment, in order to increase the productivity of labor in consonance with those principles of compulsion according to which we are constructing our whole economic life".

The experiment was made, and it gave surprising results. Whether the old "bourgeois notion" proved correct, or the newest socialism was powerless "internally, psychologically compulsory" to "draw the worker into the process of production" by means of premiums, punishment, etc., at any rate, the worker refused to be snared by the tempting formula of "psychological coercion". Evidently the ideology as well as the practice of Bolshevism convinced the toilers that the socio-economic ideals of the Bolsheviks are incidentally also a step forward in the more intensive exploitation of labor. For Bolshevism, far from saving the country from ruin and in no way improving the conditions of existence for the masses, is attempting to turn the serf of yesterday into a complete slave. How little the Communist State is concerned about the workers' well-being is seen from the statement of a prominent Communist delegate to the Tenth Congress of the Party: "Up till now Soviet policy has been characterized by the complete absence of any plan to improve the living conditions of labor". And further: "All that was done in that regard happened accidentally, or was done by fits and starts, by local authorities under pressure of the masses themselves".

Is this, then, the system of proletarian dictatorship, or State capitalism?

Chained to their work, deprived of the right to leave the job on pain of prison or summary execution for "labor desertion"; bossed and spied upon by Party overseers; divided into qualified sheep (artisans) and unqualified goats (laborers) receiving unequal food rations; hungry and insufficiently clad, deprived of the right to protest or strike — such are the modern proletarians of the Communist dictatorship. Is this "self-organization" of the toiling masses not a step backward, a return to feudal serfdom or negro slavery? Is the hand of the Communist State executioner less ruthless than the whip of the plantation boss? Only scholasticism or blind fanaticism can see in this, the most grievous form of slavery, the emancipation of labor or even the least approach to it.

It is the height of tragedy that State Socialism, enmeshed in logical antitheses, could give to the world nothing better than the intensification of the evils of the very system whose antagonisms produced socialism.

The Party dictatorship applies the same policy, in every detail, also to the peasantry. Here, too, the State is the universal master. The same policy of compulsory labor service, of oppression, spying, and systematic expropriation of the fruits of the peasant's toil: the former method of requisition which frequently stripped the peasants even of the necessaries of life; or the newly initiated, but no less predatory, food tax; tile senseless, enormous waste of foodstuffs due to the cumbrous system of centralization and the Bolshevik food policy; the dooming of whole peasant districts to slow starvation, disease and death; punitive expeditions, massacring peasant families by the wholesale and razing entire villages to the ground for the slightest resistance to the plundering policy of the Communist dictatorship—such are the methods of Bolshevik rule.

Thus, neither economic nor political exploitation of the industrial and agrarian proletariat has ceased. Only its forms have changed: formerly exploitation was purely capitalistic; now, labeled "workers' and peasants' government" and christened "communist economy", it is State capitalistic.

But this modern system of State capitalism is pernicious not only because it degrades the living human into a soulless machine. It contains another, no less destructive, element. By its very nature this system is extremely aggressive. Far from abolishing militarism, in the narrow sense of the term, it applies the principle of militarization—with all its attributes of mechanical discipline, irresponsible authority and repression—to every phase of human effort.

Socialist militarism is not only admitted, but defended and justified by the theoreticians of the Party. Thus Bukharin in his work on the "Economics of the Transition Period" writes: "The workers' government, when waging war, seeks to broaden and strengthen the economic foundations on which it is built—that is, socialist forms of production. Incidentally, it is clear from this that, in principle, even an aggressive revolutionary socialist war is permissible". And, indeed, we are already familiar with some imperialistic pretensions of the "workers" dictatorship.

Thus the "bourgeois prejudices" kicked out through the window re-enter through the door.

It is evident that the militarism of the "labor" dictatorship, like any other militarism, necessitates the formation of a gigantic army of non-producers. Moreover, such an army and all its various organs must be supplied with technical resources and means of existence, which puts additional burdens on the producers, that is, the workers and the peasants.

Another, and the most momentous internal danger, is the dictatorship itself. The dictatorship which, despotic and ruthless, has alienated itself from the laboring masses, has strangled initiative and liberty, suppressed the creative spirit of the very elements which bore the brunt of the Revolution, and is slowly but effectively instilling its poison in the hearts and minds of Russia.

Thus does the dictatorship itself sow counter-revolution. Not conspiracies from without, not the campaigns of the Denikins and Wrangels are the Damocles sword of Russia. The real and greatest danger is that country-wide disillusionment, resentment and hatred of Bolshevik despotism, that counter-revolutionary attitude of the people at large, which is the legitimate offspring of the Communist Party dictatorship itself.

Even in the ranks of the proletariat is ripening, with cumulative force, the protest against the reactionary "big stick" policy of Bolshevism.

The organized labor movement of Russia developed immediately after the February Revolution. The formation of shop and factory committees was the first step toward actual control by labor of the activities of the capitalist owners. Such control, however, could not be general without coordinating the work of all other similar committees, and thus came to life Soviets, or General Councils, of shop and factory committees, and their All-Russian Congress.

In this manner the shop and factory committees (*zahvkomy*) were the pioneers in labor control of industry, with the prospect of themselves, in the near future, managing the industries entire. The labor unions, on the other hand, were engaged in improving the living conditions and cultural environment of their membership.

But after the October Revolution the situation changed. The centralization methods of the Bolshevik dictatorship penetrated also into the unions. The autonomy of the shop committees was now declared superfluous. The labor unions were reorganized on industrial principles, with the shop committee emasculated into a mere "embryo" of the union, and entirely subjected to the authority of the central organs. Thus all independence of action, all initiative was torn from the hands of the workers themselves and transferred to the union bureaucracy. The result of this policy was the complete indifference of the workers to their unions and to the fate of the industries.

Then the Communist Party began to fill the labor unions with its own party members. They occupied the union offices. That was easily done because all the other political parties were outlawed and there existed no public press except the official Bolshevik publications. No wonder that within a short time the Communists proved an overwhelming majority in all the provincial and central executive committees, and had in their hands the exclusive management of the labor unions. They usurped the dominant role in every labor body, including even such organizations where the membership (as in the Union of Soviet Employees) is manifestly and most bitterly opposed to the BoIsheviki. Whenever an occasional union proved refractory, as the printers, for instance, and refused to yield to "internal psychological persuasion", the Communists solved the difficulty by the simple expedient of suspending the entire administration of the union.

Having gained control of the political machinery of the labor organizations, the Communist Party formed in every shop and factory small groups of its own members, so-called Communist "cells", which became the practical masters of the situation. The Communist "cell" is vested with such powers that no action of the shop or factory committee (even if the latter consist of Communists) is valid unless sanctioned by the "cell". The highest organ of the labor movement, the All-Russian Central Soviet of Labor Unions, is itself under the direct control of the Central Committee of the Communist Party.

Lenin and other Bolshevik leaders take the position that the labor union must be, first and foremost, a "school of Communism". In practice the role of the labor union in Russia is reduced to that of an automatic agency for the execution of the orders of the ruling Party.

However, this state of affairs is becoming unbearable even to that labor element which is still faithful to the commandments of State Communism. In the ranks of the Communist Party itself there has developed an opposition movement against the military governmentalization of the labor unions. This new movement, known as the Labor Opposition, though still loyal to its Communist parent, yet realizes the full horror of the hopeless position, the "blind alley" into which the criminally stupid policies of the Bolsheviks have driven the Russian proletariat and the Revolution.

The Labor Opposition is characterized by the good orthodox Communist Kolontay as "the advance guard of the proletariat, class conscious and welded by the ties of class interests", an element which "has not estranged itself from the rank and file of the working masses and has not become lost among Soviet office holders." This Labor Opposition protests "against the bureaucratization, against the differentiation between the 'upper' and the 'lower' people", against the excesses of the Party hegemony, and against the shifting and twisting policy of the ruling central power. "The great creative and constructive power of the proletariat", says the Labor Opposition, "cannot be replaced, in the task of building the Communist society, by the mere emblem of the dictatorship of the working class" — of that dictatorship which a prominent Communist characterized at the last Congress of the Communist Party as "the dictatorship of the Party bureaucracy".

Indeed, the Labor Opposition is justified in asking: "Are we, the proletariat, really the backbone of the working class dictatorship, or are we to be considered merely as a will-less herd, good enough only to carry on our backs some party politicians who are pretending to reconstruct the economic life of the country without our control, without our constructive class spirit?"

And this Labor Opposition, according to Kolontay, "keeps on growing in spite of the determined resistance on the part of the most influential leaders of the Party, and gains more and more adherents among the laboring masses throughout Russia".

But the Tenth Congress of the Communist Party of Russia (April, 1921) put its decisive veto on the Labor Opposition. Henceforth it is officially doomed, discussion of its ideas and principles forbidden because of "their Anarcho-syndicalist tendency", as Lenin expressed himself. The Communist Party declared war on the Labor Opposition. The Party Congress decided that "propagation of the principles of the Labor Opposition is incompatible with membership in the Communist Party". The demand to turn the management of the industries over to the proletariat was outlawed.

The October Revolution was initiated with the great battle cry of the First International, "The emancipation of the workers must be accomplished by the workers themselves". Yet we saw that, when the period of constructive destruction had passed, when the foundations of Tsarism had been razed, and the bourgeois system abolished, the Communist Party thought itself sufficiently strong to take into its own hands the entire management of the country. It began the education of the workers in a spirit of strictest authoritarianism, and step by step the Soviet system became transformed into a bureaucratic, punitive police machine. Terrorism became its logical, inevitable handmaid.

General indifference and hatred, and complete social paralysis, were the result of the government course. An atmosphere of slavish submission, at once revolting and disgusting, pervades the whole country. It stifles alike the oppressed and the oppressors.

What boots it that the sober-minded, compromise-ready Lenin begins his every speech with the confession of the many and serious mistakes which have been made by the Party in power? No piling up of mistakes by the "ingenious opportunist", as Lunacharsky dubs Lenin, can dismay the champions of Bolshevism intoxicated with their Party's political dominion. The mistakes of their leaders become, in the interpretation of Communist theoreticians and publicists, "eminent necessity", and the convulsive attempts to correct them (the whole agrarian policy) are hailed as acts of the greatest wisdom, humanity and loyalty to Bolshevik principles.

In vain the impatient cry of Kolontay: "The fear of criticism, inherent in our system of bureaucracy, at times reaches the point of caricature". The Party Elders brand her a heretic for her pains, her pamphlet "The Labor Opposition" is prohibited, and Ilyitch himself (Lenin) "settles" her with a few sarcastic personal slurs. The syndicalist "peril" is supposedly removed.

Meanwhile the Opposition is growing, deepening, spreading throughout working Russia.

Indeed, what shall the impartial observer think of the peculiar picture presented by Bolshevik Russia? Numerous labor strikes, with scores of workers arrested and often summarily executed; peasant uprisings and revolts, continuous revolutionary insurrections in various parts of the country. Is it not a terribly tragic situation, a heinous absurdity? Is not the rebellion of workers and peasants, however lacking in class consciousness in some cases, actual war against the workers' and peasants' government—the very government which is flesh of the flesh and blood of the blood of themselves, which had been called to guard their interests, and whose existence should be possible only in so far as it corresponds to the needs and demands of the laboring masses?

The popular protests do not cease. The opposition movement grows, and in self-defense the Party must, from time to time, mollify the people, even at the sacrifice of its principles. But where it is impossible by a few sops to still the craving for bread and liberty, the hungry mouths are shut with bullet or bayonet, and the official press brands the protestants with the infamous name of "counter-revolutionists", traitors against the "workers' and peasants' government".

Then Russia, Bolshevik Russia, is quiet again—with the quietness of death.

The history of recent days is filled with gruesome illustrations of such "quiet".

One of those illustrations is Kronstadt—Kronstadt, against which has been perpetrated the most awful crime of the Party dictatorship, a crime against the proletariat, against socialism, against the Revolution. A crime multiplied a hundredfold by the deliberate and perfidious lies spread by the Bolsheviks throughout the world.

Future history will deal adequately with this crying shame. Here we shall give but a brief sketch of the Kronstadt events.

In the month of February, 1921, the workers of four Petrograd factories went on strike. It had been an exceptionally hard winter for them: they and their families suffered from cold, hunger and exhaustion. They demanded an increase of their food rations, some fuel and clothing. Here and there was also voiced the demand for the Constituent Assembly and free trade. The strikers attempted a street demonstration, and the authorities ordered out the military against them, chiefly the *"kursants"*, the young Communists of the military training schools.

When the Kronstadt sailors learned what was happening in Petrograd, they expressed their solidarity with the strikers in their economic and revolutionary demands, but refused to support any call for the Constituent Assembly and free trade. On March 1, the sailors organized a mass-meeting in Kronstadt which was attended also by the Chairman of the All-Russian Central Executive Committee, Kalinin, (the presiding officer of the Republic of Russia), by the Commander of the Fortress of Kronstadt, Kuzmin, and by the Chairman of the Kronstadt Soviet, Vassilyev. The meeting, held with the knowledge and permission of the Executive Committee of the

Kronstadt Soviet, passed resolutions approved by the sailors, the garrison and the citizen meeting of 16,000 persons. Kalinin, Kuzmin and Vassilyev spoke against the resolutions. The main points of the latter were: free speech and free press for the revolutionary parties; amnesty for imprisoned revolutionists; re-election of the Soviets by secret ballot and freedom from government interference during the electioneering campaign.

The Bolshevik authorities replied to the resolutions by beginning to remove from the city the food and ammunition supplies. The sailors prevented the attempt, closed the entrances to the city, and arrested some of the more obstreperous commissars. Kalinin was permitted to return to Petrograd.

No sooner did the Petrograd authorities learn of the Kronstadt resolutions, than they initiated a campaign of lies and libel. In spite of the fact that Zinoviev kept in constant telephonic communication with the presiding officer of the Kronstadt Soviet, and was assured by the latter that all was quiet in Kronstadt and that the sailors were busy only with preparations for the re-elections, the Petrograd radio station was kept hard at work sending messages to the world announcing a counter-revolutionary conspiracy and a white-guard uprising in Kronstadt. At the same time Zinoviev, Kalinin and their aids succeeded in persuading the Petrograd Soviet to pass a resolution which was an ultimatum to Kronstadt to surrender immediately, on pain of complete annihilation in case of refusal.

A group of well-known and trusted revolutionists, then in Petrograd, realizing the provocative character of such a policy, appealed to Zinoviev and to the Council of Defense, of which he was the President. They pointed out the un-revolutionary, reactionary nature of his policy and its great danger to the Revolution. The demands of Kronstadt were clearly set forth: they were against the Constituent Assembly, against free trade, and in favor of the Soviet form of government. But the people of Kronstadt, as they frankly stated in their bulletin, could no longer tolerate tile despotism of the Party, and demanded the right to air their grievances and the re-establishment of free Soviets. "All power to the Soviets" was again their watch-word, as it had been that of the people and of the Bolsheviks in 1917. To resort to armed force against Kronstadt were the height of folly; indeed, a terrible crime. The only right and revolutionary solution lay in complying with the request of Kronstadt (wired by the sailors to Zinoviev, but not transmitted by him to the Soviet) for the selection of an impartial Commission to reach an amicable settlement.

But this appeal of the Petrograd group of revolutionaries was ignored. Many Communists clearly understood how maliciously reactionary was the government attitude toward Kronstadt, but slavishly debased and morally crippled by the jesuitism of the Party, they dared not speak and mutely participated in the crime.

On March 7th Trotsky began the bombardment of Kronstadt, and on the 17th the fortress and city were taken, after numerous fierce assaults involving terrific human sacrifice and treachery. Thus Kronstadt was "liquidated", and the "counter-revolutionary plot" quenched in blood. The "conquest" of the city was characterized by ruthless savagery to the defeated, although not a single one of the Communists arrested by the Kronstadt sailors had been injured or killed by them. And even before the storming of the fortress the Bolsheviks summarily executed numerous soldiers of the Red Army, whose revolutionary spirit and solidarity caused them to refuse to participate in the bloody bath.

The "conspiracy" and the "victory" were necessary for the Communist Party to save it from threatening inner decomposition. Trotsky, who during the discussion of the role of the Labor Unions (at the joint session of the Communist Party, the Central Executive Council of the Unions, and the delegates to the 6th Congress of the Soviets, December 30, 1920) was treated by Lenin as a bad boy who "don't know his Marx", once more proved himself the savior of the "country in danger". Harmony was re-established.

A few days after the "glorious conquest" of Kronstadt, Lenin said at the 10th Congress of the Communist Party of Russia: "The sailors did not want the counter-revolutionists but — they did not want us, either". And — irony of the executioner!--at that very Congress Lenin advocated free trade, "as a respite".

On March 17th the Communist government celebrated its bloody victory over the Kronstadt proletariat, and on the 18th it commemorated the martyrs of the Paris Commune. As if it was not evident to all who had eyes and would see, that the crime committed against Kronstadt was far more terrible and enormous than the slaughter of the Commune in 1871, for it was done in the name of the

Social Revolution, in the name of the Socialist Republic. Henceforth to the vile classic figures of Thiers and Gallifet are added those of Trotsky, Zinoviev, Dihbenko, Tukhachefsky.

Thus is human sacrifice brought to the Moloch of Bolshevism, to the gigantic lie that is still growing and spreading throughout the world and enmeshing it in its network of ruin, falsehood and treachery. Nor is it only the liberty and lives of individual citizens which are sacrificed to this god of clay, nor even merely the well-being of the country: it is Socialist ideals and the fate of the Revolution which are being destroyed.

Long ago Bakunin wrote: "The whole power of the Russian Tsar is built upon a lie—a lie at home and it lie abroad: a colossal and artful system of lies never witnessed before, perhaps, in the whole history of man".

But now such a system exists. It is the system of State Communism. The revolutionary proletariat of the world must open their eyes to the real situation in Russia. They should learn to see to what a terrible abyss the ruling Bolshevik Party, by its blind and bloody dictatorship, has brought Russia and the Russian Revolution. Let the world proletariat give ear to the voices of true revolutionists, the voices of those whose object is not political party power, but the success of the Social Revolution, and to whom the Revolution is synonymous with human dignity, liberty and social regeneration.

May the proletariat of Europe and America, when the world revolution comes, choose a different road than the one followed by the Bolsheviks. The road of Bolshevism leads to the formation of a social régime with new class antagonisms and class distinctions; it leads to State capitalism, which only the blind fanatic can consider as a transition stage toward a free society in which all class differences are abolished.

State Communism, the contemporary Soviet government, is not and can never become the threshold of a free, voluntary, non-authoritarian Communist society, because the very essence and nature of governmental, compulsory Communism excludes such an evolution. Its consistent economic and political centralization, its governmentalization and bureaucratization of every sphere of human activity and effort, its inevitable militarization and degradation of the human spirit mechanically destroy every germ of new life and extinguish the stimuli of creative, constructive work.

It is the Communist Party dictatorship itself which most effectively hinders the further development and deepening of the Revolution.

The historic struggle of the laboring masses for liberty necessarily and unavoidably proceeds outside the sphere of governmental influence. The struggle against oppression—political, economic and social—against the exploitation of man by man, or of the individual by the government, is always simultaneously also a struggle against government as such. The political State, whatever its form, and constructive revolutionary effort are irreconcilable. They are mutually exclusive. Every revolution in the course of its development faces this alternative: to build freely, independent and despite of the government, or to choose government with all the limitation and stagnation it involves. The path of the Social Revolution, of the constructive self-reliance of the organized, conscious masses, is in the direction of non-government, that is, of Anarchy. Not the State, not government, but systematic and coordinated social reconstruction by the toilers is necessary for the upbuilding of the new, free society. Not the State and its police methods, but the solidaric cooperation of all working elements—the proletariat, the peasantry, the revolutionary intelligentsia mutually helping each other in their voluntary associations, will emancipate us from the State superstition and bridge the passage between the abolished old civilization and Free Communism. Not by order of some central authority, but organically, from life itself, must grow up the closely-knit federation of the united industrial, agrarian, etc. associations; by the workers themselves must it be organized and managed, and then—and only then—will the great aspiration of labor for social regeneration have a sound, firm foundation. Only such an organisation of the commonwealth will make room for the really free, creative, new humanity, and will he the actual threshold of nongovernmental, Anarchist Communism.

Thus, and only thus, can be completely swept away all the remnants of our old, dying civilization, and the human mind and heart relieved of the varied poisons of ignorance and prejudice.

The revolutionary world proletariat must be permitted to hear this Anarchist voice, which cries to them—as of yore—from the depths, from the prison dungeons.

The world proletariat should understand the great tragedy of the toilers of Russia: the heart-breaking tragedy of the workers and peasants who bore the brunt of the Revolution and who find themselves now helpless in the iron clutch of an all-paralyzing State. The world proletariat must, ere too late, loosen that stranglehold.

If not, then Soviet Russia, once the hearth of the Social Revolution of the world, will again become the world's haven of blackest reaction.

Moscow, June , 1921.

The Kronstadt Rebellion

1922

I. Labor Disturbances in Petrograd

It was early in 1921. Long years of war, revolution, and civil struggle had bled Russia to exhaustion and brought her people to the brink of despair. But at last civil war was at an end: the numerous fronts were liquidated, and Wrangel—the last hope of Entente intervention and Russian counter-revolution—was defeated and his military activities within Russia terminated. The people now confidently looked forward to the mitigation of the severe Bolshevik régime. It was expected that with the end of civil war the Communists would lighten the burdens, abolish war-time restrictions, introduce some fundamental liberties, and begin the organization of a more normal life. Though far from being popular the Bolshevik Government had the support of the workers in its oft announced plan of taking up the economic reconstruction of the country as soon as military operations should cease. The people were eager to cooperate, to put their initiative and creative efforts to the reconstruction of the ruined land.

Most unfortunately, these expectations were doomed to disappointment. The Communist State showed no intention of loosening the yoke. The same policies continued, with labor militarization still further enslaving the people, embittering them with added oppression and tyranny, and in consequence paralyzing every possibility of industrial revival. The last hope of the proletariat was perishing: the conviction grew that the Communist Party was more interested in retaining political power than in saving the Revolution.

The most revolutionary elements of Russia, the workers of Petrograd, were the first to speak out. They charged that, aside from other causes, Bolshevik centralization, bureaucracy, and autocratic attitude toward the peasants and workers were directly responsible for much of the misery and suffering of the people. Many factories and mills of Petrograd had been closed, and the workers were literally starving. They called meetings to consider the situation. The meetings were suppressed by the Government. The Petrograd proletariat, who had borne the brunt of the revolutionary struggles and whose great sacrifices and heroism alone had saved the city from Yudenitch, resented the action of the Government. Feeling against the methods employed by the Bolsheviks continued to grow. More meetings were called, with the same result. The Communists would make no concessions to the proletariat, while at the same time they were offering to compromise with the capitalists of Europe and America. The workers were indignant—they became aroused. To compel the Government to consider their demands, strikes were called in the Patronny munition works, the Trubotchny and Baltiyski mills, and in the Laferm factory. Instead of talking matters over with the dissatisfied workers, the "Workers' and Peasants' Government" created a war-time *Komitet Oborony* (Committee of Defense) with Zinoviev, the most hated man in Petrograd, as Chairman. The avowed purpose of that Committee was to suppress the strike movement.

It was on February 24 that the strikes were declared. The same day the Bolsheviks sent the *kursanti*, the Communist students of the military academy (training officers for the Army and Navy), to disperse the workers who had gathered on Vassilevsky Ostrov, the labor district of Petrograd. The next day, February 25, the indignant strikers of Vassilevsky Ostrov visited the Admiralty shops and the Galernaya docks, and induced the workers there to join their protest against the autocratic attitude of the Government. The attempted street demonstration of the strikers was dispersed by armed soldiery.

On February 26 the Petrograd Soviet held a session at which the prominent Communist Lashevitch, member of the Committee of Defense and of the Revolutionary Military Soviet of the Republic, denounced the strike movement in sharpest terms. He charged the workers of the Trubotchny factory with inciting dissatisfaction, accused them of being "self-seeking labor skinners (*shkurniki*) and counter-revolutionists", and proposed that the Trubotchny factory be closed. The Executive Committee of the Petrograd Soviet (Zinoviev, Chairman) accepted the suggestion. The Trubotchny strikers were locked out and thus automatically deprived of their rations

These methods of the Bolshevik Government served still further to embitter and antagonize the workers.

Strikers' proclamations now began to appear on the streets of Petrograd. Some of them assumed a distinctly political character, the most significant of them, posted on the walls of the city February 27, reading:

"A complete change is necessary in the policies of the government. First of all, the workers and peasants need freedom. They don't want to live by the decrees of the Bolshevik: they want to control their own destinies. Comrades, preserve a revolutionary order! Determinedly and in an organized manner demand: Liberation of all arrested socialist and non-partisan workingmen; Abolition of martial law; freedom of speech, press and assembly for all who labor; Free election of shop and factory committees (*zahvkomi*), of labor union and soviet representatives. Call meetings, pass resolutions, send your delegates to the authorities and work for the realization of your demands."

The government replied to the demands of the strikers by making numerous arrests and suppressing several labor organizations. The action resulted in popular temper growing more anti-Bolshevik; reactionary slogans began to be heard. Thus on February 28 there appeared a proclamation of the "Socialist Workers of the Nevsky District", which concluded with a call for the Constituent Assembly:

"We know who is afraid of the Constituent Assembly. It is they who will no longer be able to rob the people. Instead they will have to answer before the representatives of the people for their deceit, their robberies, and their crimes. Down with the hated Communists! Down with the Soviet Government! Long live the Constituent Assembly!"

Meanwhile the Bolsheviks concentrated in Petrograd large military forces from the provinces and also ordered to the city its most trusted Communist regiments from the front. Petrograd was put under "extraordinary martial law". The strikers were overawed, and the labor unrest crushed with an iron hand.

II. The Kronstadt Movement

The Kronstadt sailors were much disturbed by what happened in Petrograd. They did not look with friendly eyes upon the Government's drastic treatment of the strikers. They knew what the revolutionary proletariat of the capital had had to bear since the first phase of the revolution, how heroically they had fought against Yudenitch, and how patiently they were suffering privation and misery. But Kronstadt was far from favoring the Constituent Assembly or the demand for free trade which made itself heard in Petrograd. The sailors were thoroughly revolutionary in spirit and action. They were the staunchest supporters of the Soviet system, but they were opposed to the dictatorship of any political party.

The sympathetic movement with the Petrograd strikers first began among the sailors of the warships *Petropavlovsk* and *Sevastopol* — the ships that in 1917 had been the main support of the Bolsheviks. The movement spread to the whole fleet of Kronstadt, then to the Red Army regiment stationed there. On February 28th the men of *Petropavlovsk* passed a resolution which was also concurred in by the sailors of *Sevastopol*. The resolution demanded, among other things, free reelection to the Kronstadt Soviet, as the tenure of office of the latter was about to expire. At the same time a committee of sailors was sent to Petrograd to learn the situation there.

On March 1 a public meeting was held on the Yakorny Square in Kronstadt, which was officially called by the crews of the First and Second Squadrons of the Baltic fleet. 16,000 sailors, Red Army men, and workers attended the gathering. It was presided over by the chairman of the Executive Committee of the Kronstadt Soviet, the Communist Vassiliev. The President of the Russian Socialist Federated Republic, Kalinin, and the Commissar of the Baltic Fleet, Kuzmin, were present and addressed the audience. It may be mentioned, as indicative of the friendly attitude of the sailors to the Bolshevik Government, that Kalinin was met on his arrival in Kronstadt with military honors, music, and banners.

At this meeting the Sailors' Committee that had been sent to Petrograd on February 28 made its report. It corroborated the worst fears of Kronstadt. The audience was outspoken in its indignation at the methods used by the Communists to crush the modest demands of the Petrograd workers. The resolution which had been passed by Petropavlovsk on February 28th was then submitted to the meeting. President Kalinin and Commissar Kuzmin bitterly attacked the resolution and denounced the Petrograd strikers as well as the Kronstadt sailors. But the arguments failed to impress the audience, and the Petropavlovsk resolution was passed unanimously. The historic document read:

"Resolution of the General Meeting of the Crews of the First and Second Squadrons of the Baltic Fleet Held March 1, 1921.

"Having heard the report of the representatives sent by the General Meeting of the Ship Crews to Petrograd to investigate the situation there, Resolved:

"(1) In view of the fact that the present Soviets do not express the will of the workers and peasants, immediately to hold new elections by secret ballot, the pre-election campaign to have full freedom of agitation among the workers and peasants; (2) To establish freedom of speech and press for workers and peasants, for Anarchists and left Socialist parties; (3) To secure freedom of assembly for labor unions and peasant organizations; (4) To call a non-partisan Conference of the workers, Red Army soldiers and sailors of Petrograd, Kronstadt, and of Petrograd Province, no later than March 10th, 1921; (5) To liberate all political prisoners of socialist parties, as well as all workers, peasants, soldiers, and sailors imprisoned in connection with the labor and peasant movements; (6) To elect a commission to review the cases of those held in prisons and concentration camps; (7) To abolish all *politotdeli* (political bureaus) because no party should be given special privileges in the propagation of its ideas or receive the financial support of the government for such purposes. Instead there should be established educational and cultural commissions, locally elected and financed by the government; (8) To abolish immediately all *zagryaditelniye otryadi* (Armed units organized by the Bolsheviks for the purpose of suppressing traffic and confiscating foodstuffs and other products. The irresponsibility and arbitrariness of their methods were proverbial throughout the country. The government abolished them in the Petrograd Province on the eve of its attack against

Kronstadt—a bribe to the Petrograd proletariat. A. B.) (9) To equalize the rations of all who work, with the exception of those employed in trades is detrimental to health; (10) To abolish the Communist fighting detachments in all branches of the Army, as well as the Communist guards kept on duty in mills and factories. Should such guards or military detachments be found necessary, they are to be appointed in the army from the ranks, and in the factories according to the judgment of the workers; (11) To give the peasants full freedom of action in regard to their land, and also the right to keep cattle, on condition that the peasants manage with their own means; that is, without employing hired labor; (12) To request all branches of the army, as well as our comrades the military *kursanti*, to concur in our resolutions; (13) To demand that the press give the fullest publicity to resolutions; (14) To appoint a Travelling Commission of Control; (15) To permit free *kustarnoye* (Individuals small scale) production by one's own efforts. Resolution passed unanimously by a brigade in meeting, two persons refraining from voting.

"Petrichenko

"Chairman Brigade Meeting

"Perepelkin

"Secretary

"Resolution passed by an overwhelming majority of the Kronstadt garrison.

"Vassilev

"Chairman

"Together with comrade Kalinin, Vassiliev votes against the resolution."

This resolution, strenuously opposed—as already mentioned—by Kalinin and Kuzmin, was passed over their protest. After the meeting Kalinin was permitted to return to Petrograd unmolested.

At the same Brigade Meeting it was also decided to send a Committee to Petrograd to explain to the workers and the garrison there the demands of Kronstadt and to request that nonpartisan delegates be sent by the Petrograd proletariat to Kronstadt to learn the actual state of affairs and the demands of the sailors. This

Committee, which consisted of thirty members, was arrested by the Bolsheviks in Petrograd. It was the first blow struck by the Communist government against Kronstadt. The fate of the Committee remained a mystery.

As the term of office of the members of the Kronstadt Soviet was about to expire, the Brigade Meeting also decided to call a Conference of delegates on March 2, to discuss the manner in which the new elections were to be held. The Conference was to consist of representatives of the ships, the garrison, the various Soviet institutions, the labor unions and factories, each organization to be represented by two delegates.

The Conference of March 2 took place in the House of Education (the former Kronstadt school of Engineering) and was attended by over 300 delegates, among whom were also Communists. The meeting was opened by the sailor Petrichenko, and a Presidium (Executive Committee) of five members of was elected *viva voce*. The main question before the delegates was the approaching new elections to the Kronstadt Soviet, to be based on more equitable principles than heretofore. The meeting was also to take action on the resolutions of March 1, and to consider ways and means of helping the country out of the desperate condition created by famine and fuel shortage.

The spirit of the Conference was thoroughly Sovietist: Kronstadt demanded Soviets free from interference by any political party; it wanted non-partisan Soviets that should truly reflect the needs and express the will of the workers and peasants. The attitude of the delegates was antagonistic to the arbitrary rule of bureaucratic commissars, but friendly to the Communist Party as such. They were staunch adherents of the Soviet system and they were earnestly seeking to find, by means friendly and peaceful, a solution of the pressing problems.

Kuzmin, Commissar of the Baltic Fleet, was the first to address the Conference. A man of more energy than judgment, he entirely failed to grasp the great significance of the moment. He was not equal to the situation: he did not know how to reach the hearts and minds of those simple men, the sailors and workers who had sacrificed so much for the Revolution and were now exhausted to the point of desperation. The delegates had gathered to take counsel with the representatives of the government. Instead Kuzmin's speech proved a firebrand thrown into gunpowder. He incensed the Conference by his arrogance and insolence. He denied the labor disorders in Petrograd, declaring that the city was quiet and the workers satisfied. He praised the work of the Commissars, questioned the revolutionary motives of Kronstadt, and warned against danger from Poland.

He stooped to unworthy insinuations and thundered threats. "If you want to open warfare", Kuzmin concluded, "you shall have it, for the Communists will not give up the reins of government. We will fight to the bitter end."

This tactless and provoking speech of the Commissar of the Baltic Fleet served to insult and outrage the delegates. The address of the Chairman of the Kronstadt Soviet, the Communist Vassiliev, who was the next speaker, made no impression on the audience: the man was colorless and indefinite. As the meeting progressed, the general attitude became more clearly anti-Bolshevik. Still the delegates were hoping to reach some friendly understanding with the representatives of the government. But presently it became apparent, states the official report, that "we could not trust comrades Kuzmin and Vassiliev anymore, and that it was necessary to detain them temporarily, especially because the Communists were in possession of arms, and we had no access to the telephones. The soldiers stood in fear of the Commissars, as proved by the letter read at the meeting, and the Communists did not permit gatherings of the garrison to take place."

Kuzmin and Vassiliev were therefore removed from the meeting and placed under arrest. It is characteristic of the spirit of the Conference that the motion to detain the other Communists present was voted down by an overwhelming majority. The delegates held the Communists must be considered on equal footing with the representatives of other organizations and accorded the same rights and treatment. Kronstadt still was determined to find some bond of agreement with the Communist Party and the Bolshevik Government.

The resolutions of March 1 were read and enthusiastically passed. At that moment the Conference was thrown into great excitement by the declaration of a delegate that the Bolsheviks were about to attack the meeting and that fifteen carloads of soldiers and Communists, armed with rifles and machine guns, had been dispatched for that purpose. "This information", the *Izvestia* report continues, "produced passionate resentment among the delegates. Investigation soon proved the report groundless, but rumors persisted that a regiment of *kursanti*, headed by the notorious Tchekist Dukiss, was already marching in the direction of the Fort Krasnaia Gorka". In view of these new developments, and remembering the threats of Kuzmin and Kalinin, the Conference at once took up the question of organizing the defense of Kronstadt against Bolshevik attack. Time pressing, it was decided to turn the Presidium of the Conference into a Provisional Revolutionary Committee, which was charged with the duty of preserving the order and safety of the city. That committee was also to make the necessary preparations for holding the new elections to the Kronstadt Soviet.

III. Bolsheviks campaign against Kronstadt

Petrograd was in a state of high nervous tension. New strikes had broken out and there were persistent rumors of labor disorders in Moscow, of peasant uprisings in the East and in Siberia. For lack of a reliable public press the people gave credence to the most exaggerated and even to obviously false reports. All eyes were on Kronstadt in expectation of momentous developments.

The Bolsheviks lost no time in organizing their attack against Kronstadt. Already on March 2 the Government issued a *prikaz* (order) signed by Lenin and Trotsky, which denounced the Kronstadt movement as in mutiny against the Communist authorities. In that document the sailors were charged with being "the tools of former Tsarist generals who together with Socialist-Revolutionary traitors staged a counter-revolutionary conspiracy against the proletarian Republic". The Kronstadt movement for free Soviets was characterized by Lenin and Trotsky as "the work of Entente interventionists and French spies". "On February 28", the *prikaz* read, "there were passed by the men of the Petropavlovsk resolutions breathing the spirit of the Black Hundreds. Then there appeared on the scene the group of the former general, Kozlovsky. He and three of his officers, whose names we have not yet ascertained, have openly assumed the role of rebellion. Thus the meaning of recent events has become evident. Behind the Socialist-Revolutionists again stands a Tsarist general. In view of all this the Council of Labor and Defense orders: (1) To declare the former general Kozlovsky and his aides outlawed; (2) To put the City of Petrograd and the Petrograd Province under martial law; (3) To place supreme power over the whole

Petrograd District into the hands of the Petrograd Committee of Defense."

There was indeed a former general, Kozlovsky, in Kronstadt. It was Trotsky who had placed him there as an Artillery specialist. He played no role whatever in the Kronstadt events, but the Bolsheviks clearly exploited his name to denounce the sailors as enemies of the Soviet Republic and their movement as counterrevolutionary. The official Bolshevik press now began its campaign of calumny and defamation of Kronstadt as a hotbed of "White conspiracy headed by General Kozlovsky", and Communist agitators were sent among the workers in the mills and factories of Petrograd and Moscow to call upon the proletariat "to rally to the support and defense of the Workers and Peasants Government against the counter-revolutionary uprising in Kronstadt".

Far from having anything to do with generals and counter-revolutionists, the Kronstadt sailors refused to accept aid even from the Socialist-Revolutionist Party. Its leader, Victor Tchernov, then in Reval, attempted to influence the sailors in favor of his Party and its demands, but received no encouragement from the Provisional Revolutionary Committee. Tchernov sent to Kronstadt the following radio message:

"The Chairman of the Constituent Assembly, Victor Tchernov, sends his fraternal greetings to the heroic comrades-sailors, the Red Army men and workers, who for the third time since 1905 are throwing off the yoke of tyranny. He offers to aid with men and to provision Kronstadt through the Russian cooperatives abroad. Inform what and how much is needed. Am prepared to come in person and give my energies and authority to the service of the people's revolution. I have faith in the final victory of the laboring masses. Hail to the first to raise the banner of the People's Liberation! Down with despotism from the left and right!"

At the same time the Socialist-Revolutionist Party sent the following message to Kronstadt: "The Socialist-Revolutionist delegation abroad, now that cup of the People's wrath is overflowing, offers to help with all means in its power in the struggle for liberty and popular government. Inform in what ways help is desired. Long live the people's revolution! Long live free Soviets and the Constituent Assembly!"

The Kronstadt Rrevolutionary Committee declined the Socialist-Revolutionist offers. It sent the following reply to Victor Tchernov: "The provisional Revolutionary Committee of Kronstadt expresses to all our brothers abroad its deep gratitude for their sympathy. The Provisional Revolutionary Committee is thankful for the offer of Comrade Tchernov, but refrains for the present: that is, till further developments become clarified. Meantime everything will be taken into consideration

"Petrichenko, Chairman, Provisional Revolutionary Committee"

Moscow, however, continued its campaign of misrepresentation. On March 3 the Bolshevik radio station sent out the following message to the world (certain parts undecipherable owing to interference from another station): "That the armed uprising of the former general Kozlovsky has been organized by the spies of the Entente, like many similar previous plots, is evident from the bourgeois French newspaper *Matin*, which two weeks prior to the Kozlovsky rebellion published the following telegram from Helsingfors: 'As a result of the recent Kronstadt uprising the Bolshevik military authorities have taken steps to isolate Kronstadt and to prevent the sailors and soldiers of Kronstadt from entering Petrograd.' It is clear that the Kronstadt uprising was made in Paris and organized by the French secret service. The Socialist-Revolutionists, also controlled and directed from Paris, have been preparing rebellions against the Soviet Government, and no sooner were their preparations made than there appeared the real master, the Tsarist general."

The character of the numerous other messages sent by Moscow can be judged by the following radio: "Petrograd is orderly and quiet, and even a few factories where accusations against the Soviet Government were recently voiced now understand that it is the work of provocateurs. They realize where the agents of the Entente and of counter-revolution are leading them to. Just at this moment, when in America a new Republican régime is assuming the reins of government and showing inclination to take up business relations with Soviet Russia, the spreading of lying rumors and the organization of disturbances in Kronstadt have the sole purpose of influencing the new American President and changing his policy toward Russia. At the same time the London Conference is holding its sessions, and the spreading of similar rumors must influence also the

Turkish delegation and make it more submissive to the demands of the Entente. The rebellion of the Petropavlovsk crew is undoubtedly part of a great conspiracy to create trouble within Soviet Russia and to injure our international position. This plan is being carried out within Russia by a Tsarist general and former officers, and their activities are supported by the Mensheviks and Socialist-Revolutionists."

The Petrograd committee of defense, directed by Zinoviev, its chairman, assumed full control of the city and Province of Petrograd. The whole Northern District was put under martial law and all meetings prohibited. Extraordinary precautions were taken to protect the Government institutions and machine guns were placed in the Astoria, the hotel occupied by Zinoviev and other high Bolshevik functionaries. The proclamations posted on the street bulletin boards ordered the immediate return of all strikers to the factories, prohibited suspension of work, and warned the people against congregating on the streets. "In such cases", the order read, "the soldiery will resort to arms. In case of resistance, shooting on the spot".

The committee of defense took up the systematic "cleaning of the city". Numerous workers, soldiers and sailors suspected of sympathizing with Kronstadt, were placed under arrest. All Petrograd sailors and several Army regiments thought to be "politically untrustworthy" were ordered to distant points, while the families of Kronstadt sailors living in Petrograd were taken into custody as hostages. The Committee of Defense notified Kronstadt of its action by proclamation scattered over the city from an aeroplane on March 4, which stated: "The Committee of Defense declares that the arrested are held as hostages for the Commissar of the Baltic Fleet, N. N. Kuzmin, the Chairman of the Kronstadt Soviet, T. Vassiliev, and other Communists. If the least harm be suffered by our detained comrades, the hostages will pay with their lives".

"We do not want bloodshed. Not a single Communists has been shot by us", was Kronstadt's reply.

IV. The Aims of Kronstadt

Kronstadt revived with the new life. Revolutionary enthusiasm rose to a level of the October days when the heroism and devotion of the saliors played such a decisive role. Now for the first time since the Communist Party assumed exclusive control of the Revolution and the fate of Russia, Kronstadt felt itself free. A new spirit of solidarity and brotherhood brought the sailors, the soldiers of the garrison, the factory workers, and the nonpartisan elements together in united effort for their common cause. Even Communists were affected by the fraternalization of the whole city and joined in the work preparatory to the approaching elections to the Kronstadt Soviet.

Among the first steps taken by the Provisional Revolutionary Committee was the preservation of revolutionary order in Kronstadt and the publication of the Committee's official organ, the daily *Izvestia*. Its first appeal to the people of Kronstadt (issue No. 1, March 3, 1921) was thoroughly characteristic of the attitude and temper of the sailors. "The revolutionary committee", it read, "is most concerned that no blood be shed. It has exerted its best efforts to organize revolutionary order in the city, the fortress and the forts. Comrades and citizens, do not suspend work! Workers, remain at your machines; sailors and soldiers, be on your posts. All Soviet employees and institutions should continue their labors. The Provisional Revolutionary Committee calls upon you all, comrades and citizens, to give it your support and aid. Its mission is to organize, the fraternal cooperation with you, the conditions necessary for honest and just elections to the new Soviet".

The pages of the *Izvestia* bear abundant witness to the deep faith of the Revolutionary Committee in the people of Kronstadt and their aspirations towards the free Soviets as the true road of liberation from the oppression of Communist bureaucracy. In its daily organ and radio messages the Revolutionary Committee indignantly resented the Bolshevik campaign of calumny and repeatedly appealed to the proletariat of Russia and of the world for understanding, sympathy, and help. The radio of March 6 sounds the keynote of Kronstadt's call:

"Our cause is just: we stand for the power of Soviets, not parties. We stand for freely elected representatives of the laboring masses. The substitutes Soviets manipulated by the Communist Party have always been deaf to our needs and demands; the only reply we have ever received was shooting.

"Comrades! They not only deceive you: they deliberately pervert the truth and resort to most despicable defamation.

"In Kronstadt the whole power is exclusively in the hands of the revolutionary sailors, soldiers and workers—not with the counter-revolutionists led by some Kozlovsky, as the lying Moscow Radio tries to make you believe.

"Do not delay, comrades! Join us, get in touch with us: demand admission to Kronstadt for your delegates. Only they will tell you the whole truth and expose the fiendish calumny about Finnish bread and Entente offers. Long live the revolutionary proletariat and the peasantry! Long live the power of freely elected Soviets!"

The Provisional Revolutionary Committee first had its headquarters on the flagship *Petropavlovsk*, but within a few days it removed to the "People's Home", in the center of Kronstadt, in order to be, as the *Izvestia* states, "in closer touch with the people and make access to the Committee easier than on the ship". Although the Communist press continued its turbulent denunciation of Kronstadt as "the counter-revolutionary rebellion of the General Kozlovsky", the truth of the matter was that the Revolutionary Committee was exclusively proletarian, consisting for the most part of workers of known revolutionary record.

Not without a sense of humor did the Kronstadt *Izvestia* remark in this connection: "These are our generals, Messrs. Trotsky and Zinoviev, while the Brussilovs, the Kamenevs, the Tukhachevskis, and the other celebrities of the Tsar's régime are on your side."

The Provisional Revolutionary Committee enjoyed the confidence of the whole population of Kronstadt. It won general respect by establishing and firmly adhering to the principle of "equal rights for all, privileges to none". The *pahyok* (food ration) was equalized. The sailors, who under Bolshevik rule always received rations far in excess of those allotted to the workers, themselves voted to accept no more than the average citizen and toiler. Special rations and delicacies were given only to hospitals and children's homes.

The just and generous attitude of the Revolutionary Committee towards the Kronstadt members of the Communist Party—few of whom had been arrested in spite of Bolshevik repressions and all holding of sailors' families as hostages—won the respect even of the Communists. The pages of *Izvestia* contain numerous communications from Communist groups and organizations of Kronstadt, condemning the attitude of the Central Government and indorsing the stand and measures of the Provisional Revolutionary Committee. Many Kronstadt Communists publicly announced their withdrawal from the Party as a protest against its despotism and bureaucratic corruption. In various issues of the *Izvestia* there are to be found hundreds of names of Communists whose conscience made it impossible for them to "remain in the Party of the executioner Trotsky", as some of them expressed it. Resignations from the Communist Party soon became so numerous as to resemble a general exodus. The following letters, taken at random from a large batch, sufficiently characterize the sentiment of the Kronstadt Communists:

"(1) I have come to realize that the policies of the Communist Party have brought the country into a hopeless blind alley from which there is no exit. The Party has become bureaucratic, it has learned nothing and it does not want to learn. It refuses to listen to the voice of a 115 million peasants; it does not want to consider that only freedom of speech and opportunity to participate in the reconstruction of the country, by means of altered election methods, can bring our country out of its lethargy. I refused henceforth to consider myself a member of the Russian Communist Party. I wholly approve of the resolution passed by the all-city meeting on March 1, and I hereby place my energies and abilities at the disposal of the Provisional Revolutionary Committee."

"(2) Comrades, my pupils of the industrial, Red Army, and naval schools! Almost thirty years I have lived in deep love for the people, and have carried light and knowledge, so far as lay in my power, to all who thirsted for it, up to the present moment.

"The Revolution of 1917 gave greater scope to my work, increased my activities, and I devoted myself with greater energy to the service of my ideal.

"The communist slogan, 'All for the people', inspired me with its nobility and beauty, and in February, 1920, I entered the Russian Communist Party as a candidate. But the "first shot" fired at the peaceful population, at my dearly beloved children of which there are about seven thousand in Kronstadt, fills me with horror that I may be considered as sharing responsibility for the blood of the innocents thus shed. I feel that I can no longer believe in and propagate that which has disgraced itself by fiendish act. Therefore with the first shot I have ceased to regard myself as a member of the Communist Party."

Such communications appeared in almost every issue of the *Izvestia*. Most significant was the declaration of the Provisional Bureau of the Kronstadt Section of the Communist Party, whose Manifesto to its members was published in the *Izvestia*, No. 2, March 4th:

"Let every comrade of our Party realize the importance of the present hour.

"Give no credence to the false rumors that Communists are being shot, and that the Kronstadt Communists are about to rise up in arms. Such rumors are spread to cause bloodshed.

"We declare that our Party has always been defending the conquests of the working-class against all known and secret enemies of the power of the workers' and peasants' Soviets, and will continue to do so.

"The Provisional Bureau of the Kronstadt Communist Party recognizes the necessity for elections to the Soviet and calls upon the members of the Communist Party to take part in the elections.

"The Provisional Bureau of the Communist Party directs all members of the Party to remain at their posts and in no way to obstruct or interfere with the measures of the Provisional Revolutionary Committee.

"Long live the power of the Soviets! Long live the international union of workers!"

Similarly, various other organizations, civil and military, expressed their opposition to the Moscow régime and their entire agreement with the demands of the Kronstadt sailors. Many resolutions to that effect were also passed by Red Army regiments stationed in Kronstadt and on duty in the forts. The following is expressive of their general spirit and tendency:

"We, Red Army soldiers of the Fort Krasnoarmeetz, stand wholly with the Provisional Revolutionary Committee, and to the last moment we will defend the Revolutionary Committee, the workers and peasants.

"Let no one believe the lies of the Communist proclamations thrown from aeroplanes. We have no generals here and no Tsarist officers. Kronstadt has always been the city of workers and peasants, and so it will remain. The generals are in the service of the Communists.

"At this moment, when the fate of the country is in the balance, we who have taken power into our own hands and who have entrusted the Revolutionary Committee with leadership in the fight — we declare to the whole garrison and to the workers that we are prepared to die for the liberty of the laboring masses. Freed from the three-year old Communist yoke and terror we shall die rather than recede a single step. Long live Free Russia of the Working People!"

Kronstadt was inspired by passionate love of a Free Russia and unbounded faith in true Soviets. It was confident of gaining the support of the whole of Russia, of Petrograd in particular, thus bringing about the final liberation of the country. The Kronstadt *Izvestia* reiterates this attitude and hope, and in the numerous articles and appeals it seeks to clarify its position towards the Bolsheviks and its aspiration to lay the foundation of a new, free life for itself and the rest of Russia. This great aspiration, the purity of its motives, and its fervent hope of liberation standout in striking relief on the pages of the official organ of the Kronstadt Provisional Revolutionary Committee and thoroughly express the spirit of the soldiers, sailors and workers. The virulent attacks of the Bolshevik press, the infamous lies sent broadcast by the Moscow radio station accusing Kronstadt of counter-revolution and White conspiracy, the Revolutionary Committee replied to in a dignified manner. It often reproduced in its organ the Moscow proclamations in order to show to the people of Kronstadt to what depths the Bolsheviks had sunk. Occasionally the Communist methods where exposed and characterized by the *Izvestia* with just indignation, as in its issue of March 8, (No. 6), under the heading "We and They":

"Not knowing how to retain the power that is falling from their hands, the Communists resort to the vilest provocative means. Their contemptible press has mobilized all its forces to incite the masses and put the Kronstadt movement in the light of White guard conspiracy. Now a clique of shameless villains has sent word to the world that 'Kronstadt has sold itself to Finland'. Their newspapers spit fire and poison, and because they have failed to persuade the proletariat that Kronstadt is in the hands of counter-revolutionists, they are now trying to play on the nationalistic feelings.

"The whole world already knows from our radios what the Kronstadt garrison and workers are fighting for. But the Communists are striving to pervert the meaning of events and thus mislead our Petrograd brothers.

"Petrograd is surrounded by the bayonets of the *kursanti* and the Party 'guards', and *Maliuta Skuratov*—Trotsky—does not permit the delegates of the nonpartisan workers and soldiers to go to Kronstadt. He fears they would learn the whole truth there, and that truth would immediately sweep the Communists away and thus enlightened laboring masses would take the power into their own brawny hands.

"That is the reason that the Petro-Soviet (Soviet of Petrograd) did not reply to our radio telegram in which we asked that really impartial comrades be sent to Kronstadt.

"Fearing for their own skins, the leaders of the Communists suppress the truth and disseminate the lie that White Guardists are active in Kronstadt, that the Kronstadt proletariat has sold itself to Finland and to French spies, that the Finns have already organized an army in order to attack Petrograd with the aid of the *Kronstadtmyatezhnbiki* mutineers and so forth.

"To all this we can reply only this: all power to the Soviets! Keep your hands off them, the hands that are red with the blood of the martyrs of liberty who have died fighting against the White Guardists, the landlords, and the bourgeoisie!"

In simple and frank speech Kronstadt sought to express the will of the people yearning for freedom and for the opportunity to shape their own destinies. It felt itself the advance guard, so to speak, of the proletariat of Russia about to rise in defense of the great aspirations for which the people that fought and suffered in the October Revolution. The faith of the Kronstadt in the Soviet system was deep and firm; its all-inclusive slogan, "All power to the Soviets, not to parties!" That was its program; it did not have time to develop it or to theorize. It strove for the emancipation of the people from the Communist yoke. That yoke, no longer a bearable, made a new revolution, the Third Revolution, necessary. The road to liberty and peace lay in freely elected Soviets, "the cornerstone of the new revolution ". The pages of the *Izvestia* bear rich testimony to the unspoiled directness and single-mindedness of the Kronstadt sailors and workers, and the touching faith they had in their mission as the initiators of the Third Revolution. These aspirations and hopes are clearly set forth in No. 6 of the *Izvestia*, March 8, in the leading editorial entitled "What We Are Fighting For":

"With the October Revolution the working class had hoped to achieve its emancipation. But there resulted an even greater enslavement of human personality.

"The power of the police and gendarme monachy fell into the hands of usurpers—the Communists—who, instead of giving the people liberty, have instilled in them only the constant fear of the Tcheka, which by its horrors surpasses even the gendarme régime of Tsarism. Worst and most cruel of all is the spiritual cabal of the Communists: they have laid their hands also on the internal world of the laboring masses, compelling everyone to think according to Communist prescription.

"Russia of the toilers, the first to raise the red banner of labor's emancipation, is drenched with the blood of those martyred for the greater glory of Communist dominion. In that sea of blood, the Communists are drowning all the bright promises and possibilities of the workers' revolution. It has now become clear that the Russian Communist Party is not the defender of the laboring masses, as it pretends to be. The interests of the working people are foreign to it. Having gained power, it is now fearful only of losing it, and therefore it considers all means permissible: defamation, deceit, violence, murder, and vengeance upon the families of the rebels.

"There is an end to long, suffering patience. Here and there the land is lit up by the fires of rebellion in a struggle against oppression and violence. Strikes of workers have multiplied, but the Bolshevik police régime has taken every precaution against the outbreak of the inevitable Third Revolution.

"But in spite of it all it has come, and it is made by the hands of laboring masses. The Generals of Communism see clearly that it is the people who have risen, the people who have become convinced that the Communists have betrayed the ideas of Socialism. Fearing for their safety and knowing that there is no place they can hide in from the wrath of the workers, the Communists still try to terrorize the rebels with prison, shooting, and other barbarities. But life under the Communist dictatorship is more terrible than death.

"There is no middle road. To triumph or to die! The example is being set by Kronstadt, the terror of counter-revolution from the right to and from the left. Here has taken place the great revolutionary deed. Here is raised the banner of rebellion against a three-year old tyranny and oppression of Communist autocracy, which has put in the shade the three-hundred-year old despotism of monarchism. Here, in Kronstadt, has been laid the cornerstone of the Third Revolution which is to break the last chains of the worker and open the new, broad road to Socialist creativity.

"This new revolution will rouse the masses of the East and the West, and will serve as an example of new Socialist constructiveness, in contradistinction to the governmental, cut-and-dried Communist 'construction'. The laboring masses will learn that what has been done till now in the name of the workers and peasants was not Socialism.

Without firing a single shot, without shedding a drop of blood, the first step has been taken. Those who labor need no blood. They will shed it only in self-defense. The workers and peasants march on: they are leaving behind them the *utchredilka* (Constituent Assembly) with its bourgeois régime and the Communist Party dictatorship with its Tcheka and State capitalism, which has put the noose around the neck of the workers and threaten to strangle them to death.

"The present change offers the laboring masses the opportunity of securing, at last, freely elected Soviets which will function without fear of the Party whip; they can now reorganize the governmentalized labor unions into voluntary associations of workers, peasants, and working intelligentsia. At last is broken the police club of Communist autocracy."

That was the program, those the immediate demands, for which the Bolshevik government began the attack of Kronstadt at 6:45 P.M., March 7th, 1921.

V. Bolshevik Ultimatum to Kronstadt

Kronstadt was generous. Not a drop of Communist blood did it shed, in spite of all the provocation, the blockade of the city and repressive measures on the part of the Bolshevik Government. It scorned to imitate the Communist example of vengeance, even going to the extent of warning the Kronstadt population not to be guilty of excesses against members of the Communist party. The Provisional Revolutionary Committee issued a call to the people of Kronstadt to that effect, even after the Bolshevik Government had ignored the demand of the sailors for the liberation of hostages taken in Petrograd. The Kronstadt demand sent by radio to the Petrograd

Soviet and the Manifesto of the Revolutionary Committee were published on the same day, March 7, and are hereby reproduced:

"In the name of the Kronstadt garrison the Provisional Revolutionary Committee of Kronstadt demands that the families of the sailors, workers and Red Army men held by the Petro-Soviet as hostages be liberated within 24 hours.

"The Kronstadt garrison declares that the Communists enjoy full liberty in Kronstadt and their families are absolutely safe. The example of the Petro-Soviet will not be followed here, because we consider such methods (the taking of hostages) most shameful and vicious even if prompted by desperate fury. History knows no such infamy."

The Manifesto to the people of Kronstadt read in part:

"The long continued oppression of the laboring masses by the Communist dictatorship has produced very natural indignation and resentment on the part of the people. As a result of it relatives of Communists have in some instances been discharged from their positions and boycotted. That must not be. We do not seek vengeance — we are defending our labor interests."

Kronstadt lived in the spirit of its holy crusade. It had abiding faith in the justice of its cause and felt itself the true defender of the Revolution. In this state of mind the sailors did not believe that the Government would attack them by force of arms. In the subconsciousness of these simple children of the soil and sea there perhaps germinated the feeling that not only through violence may victory be gained. The Slavic psychology seemed to believe that the justice of the cause and the strength of the revolutionary spirit must win. At any rate, Kronstadt refuses to take the offensive. The Revolutionary Committee would not accept the insistent advice of the military experts to make an immediate landing in Oranienbaum, a fort of great strategic value. The Kronstadt sailors and soldiers aimed to establish free Soviets and were willing to defend their rights against attack; but they would not be the aggressors.

In Petrograd there were persistent rumors that the Government was preparing military operations against Kronstadt, but the people did not credit such stories: the thing seem so outrageous as to be absurd. As already mentioned, the Committee of Defense (officially known as the Soviet of Labour and Defense) had declared the capital to be in an "extraordinary state of siege". No assemblies were permitted, no gathering on the streets. The Petrograd workers knew little of what was transpiring in Kronstadt, the only information accessible being the Communist press and the frequent bulletins to the fact that the "Tsarist General Kozlovsky organized a counter-revolutionary uprising in Kronstadt". Anxiously the people looked forward to the announced session of the Petrograd Soviet which was to take action in the Kronstadt matter.

The Petro-Soviet met on March 4, admission being by cards which, as a rule, only Communists could procure. The writer, then on friendly terms with the Bolsheviks and particularly with Zinoviev, was present. As chairman of the Petrograd Soviet Zinoviev opened the session and in a long speech set forth the Kronstadt situation. I confess that I came to the meeting disposed rather in favor of the Zinoviev viewpoint: I was on my guard against the vaguest possibility of counter-revolutionary influence in Kronstadt. But Zinoviev's speech itself convinced me that the Communist accusations against the sailors were pure fabrication, without scintilla of truth. I had heard Zinoviev on several previous occasions. I found him a convincing Speaker, once his premises were admitted. But now his whole attitude, his argumentation, his tone and manner—all gave the lie to his words. I could sense his own conscience protesting. The only "evidence" presented against Kronstadt was the famous resolution on March 1, the demands of which were just and even moderate. It was on the sole basis of that document, supported by the vehement, almost hysterical denunciations of the sailors by Kalinin, that the fatal step was taken. Prepared beforehand and presented by the stentorian-voiced Yevdokimov, the right-hand man of Zinoviev, the resolution against Kronstadt was passed by the delegates wrought up to a high pitch of intolerance and blood thirst—passed amid a tumult of protest from several delegates of Petrograd factories and the spokesmen of the sailors. The resolution declared Kronstadt guilty of a counter-revolutionary uprising against the Soviet power and demanded its immediate surrender.

It was a declaration of war. Even many Communists refused to believe that the resolution would be carried out: it were a monstrous thing to attack by force of arms the "pride and glory of the Russian Revolution", as Trotsky had christened the Kronstadt sailors. In the circle of their friends many sober-minded Communists threatened to resign from the Party should such a bloody deed come to pass.

Trotsky had been expected to address the Petro-Soviet, and his failure to appear was interpreted by some as indicating that the seriousness of the situation was exaggerated. But during the night he arrived in Petrograd and the following morning, March 5, he issued his ultimatum to Kronstadt:

"The Workers and Peasants Government has decreed that the Kronstadt and the rebellious ships must immediately submit to the authority of the Soviet Republic. Therefore I command all who have raised their hand against the Socialist fatherland to lay down their arms at once. The obdurate are to be disarmed and turned over to the Soviet authorities. The arrested Commissars and other representatives of the Government are to be liberated at once. Only those surrendering unconditionally may count on the mercy of the Soviet Republic.

"Simultaneously I am issuing orders to prepare to quell the mutiny and subdue the mutineers by force of arms. Responsibility for the harm that may be suffered by the peaceful population will fall entirely upon the heads of the counter-revolutionary mutineers. This warning is final."

The situation looked ominous. Great military forces continuously flowed into Petrograd and its environs. Trotsky's ultimatum was followed by a *prikaz* which contained the historic threat, "I'll shoot you like pheasants". A group of Anarchists then in Petrograd made a last attempt to induce the Bolsheviks to reconsider their decision of attacking Kronstadt. They felt it their duty to the Revolution to make an effort, even if hopeless, to prevent the imminent massacre of the revolutionary flower of Russia, the Kronstadt sailors and workers. On March 5 they sent a protest to the Committee of Defense, pointing out the peaceful intentions and just demands of Kronstadt, reminding the Communists of the heroic revolutionary history of the sailors, and suggesting a method of settling the dispute in a manner befitting comrades and revolutionists. The document read:

"To the Petrograd Soviet of Labour and Defense Chairman Zinoviev:

"To remain silent now is impossible, even criminal. Recent events impel us Anarchists to speak out and to declare our attitude in the present situation. The spirit of ferment and dissatisfaction manifest among the workers and sailors is the result of causes that demand our serious attention. Cold and hunger have produced disaffection, and the absence of any opportunity for discussion and criticism is forcing the workers and sailors to air their grievances in the open.

"White-Guardist bands wish and may try to exploit this dissatisfaction in their own class interests. Hiding behind the workers and sailors they throw out slogans of the Constituent Assembly, of free trade, and similar demands.

"We Anarchists have long since exposed the fiction of these slogans, and we declare to the whole world that we will fight with arms against any counter-revolutionary attempt, in cooperation with all friends of the Soviet Revolution and hand in hand with the Bolsheviks.

"Concerning the conflict between the Soviet Government and the workers and sailors, our opinion is that it must be settled not by force of arms but by means of comradely, fraternal revolutionary agreement. Resorting to bloodshed, on the part of the Soviet Government, will not—in the given situation—intimidate or quieten the workers. On the contrary, it will serve only to aggravate matters and will strengthen the hands of the Entente and of internal counter-revolution. More important still, the use of force by the Workers and Peasants Government against workers and sailors will have a reactionary effect upon the international revolutionary movement and will everywhere result in incalculable harm to the Social Revolution. Comrades Bolsheviks, bethink yourselves before it too late! Do not play with fire: you are about to make a most serious and decisive step. We hereby submit to you the following proposition: Let a Commission be selected to consist of five persons, inclusive of two Anarchists. The Commission is to go to Kronstadt to settle the dispute by peaceful means. In the given situation this is the most radical method. It will be of international revolutionary significance."

Zinoviev informed that a document in connection with the Kronstadt problem was to be submitted to the Soviet of Defense, sent his personal representative for it. Whether the letter was discussed by that body is not known to the writer. At any rate, no action was taken in the matter.

VI. The First Shot

Kronstadt, heroic and generous, was dreaming of liberating Russia by the Third Revolution which it felt proud to have initiated. It formulated no definite program. Liberty and universal brotherhood were its slogans. It thought of the Third Revolution as a gradual process of emancipation, the first step in that direction being the free election of independent Soviets, uncontrolled by any political party and expressive of the will and interests of the people. The wholehearted, unsophisticated sailors were proclaiming to the workers of the world their great Ideal, and calling upon the proletariat to join forces in the common fight, confident that their Cause would find enthusiastic support and that workers at Petrograd, first and foremost, would hasten to their aid.

Meanwhile Trotsky had collected his forces. The most trusted divisions from the fronts, *kursanti* regiments, Tcheka detachments, and military units consisting exclusively of Communists were now gathered in the forts of Sestroretsk, Lissy Noss, Krasnaia Gorka, and neighboring fortified places. The greatest Russian military experts were rushed to the scene to form plans for the blockade and attack of Kronstadt, and the notorious Tukhachevski was appointed Commander-in-Chief in the siege of Kronstadt.

On March 7, at 6:45 in the evening, the Communist batteries of Sestroretsk and Lissy Noss fired the first shots against Kronstadt.

It was the anniversary of the Woman Workers' Day. Kronstadt, besieged and attacked, did not forget the great holiday. Under fire of numerous batteries, the brave sailors sent a radio greeting to the workingwomen of the world, an act most characteristic of the psychology of the Rebel City. The radio read:

"Today is a universal holiday—Women Workers' Day. We of Kronstadt send, amid the thunder of cannon, our fraternal greetings to workingwomen of the world. May you soon accomplish your liberation from every form of violence and oppression. Long live the free revolutionary workingwomen! Long live the Social Revolution throughout the world!"

No less characteristic was the heart rending cry of Kronstadt, "Let The Whole World Know", published after the first shot had been fired, in No. 6 of the *Izvestia*, March 8:

"The first shot has been fired. Standing up to his knees in the blood of the workers, Marshal Trotsky was the first to open fire against revolutionary Kronstadt which has risen against the autocracy of the Communists to establish the true power of the Soviets.

"Without shedding a drop of blood we, Red Army men, sailors, and workers of Kronstadt have freed ourselves from the yoke of the Communists and have even preserved their lives. By the threat of artillery they want now to subject us again to their tyranny.

"Not wishing bloodshed, we asked that nonpartisan delegates of the Petrograd proletariat be sent to us, that they may learn that Kronstadt is fighting for the Power of the Soviets. But the Communists have kept our demand from the workers of Petrograd and now they have opened fire—the usual reply of the pseudo Workers' and Peasants' Government to the demands of the laboring masses.

"But the workers of the whole world know that we, the defenders of the Soviet Power, are guarding the conquest of the Social Revolution.

"We will win or perish beneath the ruins of Kronstadt, fighting for the just cause of the laboring masses.

"The workers of the world will be our judges. The blood of the innocent will fall upon the heads of the Communist fanatics drunk with the authority.

"Long live the Power of the Soviets!"

VII. The Defeat of Kronstadt

The artillery bombardment of Kronstadt, which began on the evening of March 7, was followed by the attempt to take the fortress by storm. The attack was made from the north and south by picked Communist troops clad in white shrouds, the color of which protectively blended with the snow lying thick on the frozen Gulf of Finland. These first terrible attacks to take the fortress by storm, at the reckless sacrifice of life, are mourned by the sailors in touching commiseration for their brothers in arms, duped into believing Kronstadt counter-revolutionary. Under date of March 8th the Kronstadt *Izvestia* wrote:

"We did not want to shed the blood of our brothers, and we did not fire a single shot until compelled to do so. We had to defend the just cause of the laboring people and to shoot—to shoot at our own brothers sent to certain death by Communists who have grown fat at the expense of the people.

"To your misfortune there broke a terrific snowstorm and black night shrouded everything in darkness. Nevertheless, the Communist executioners, counting no cost, drove you along the ice, threatening you in the rear with their machine guns operated by Communist detachments.

"Many of you perished that night on the icy vastness of the Gulf of Finland. And when day broke and the storm quieted down, only pitiful remnants of you, worn and hungry, hardly able to move, came to us clad in your white shrouds.

"Early in the morning there were already about a thousand of you and later in the day a countless number. Dearly you have paid with your blood for this adventure, and after your failure Trotsky rushed back to Petrograd to drive new martyrs to slaughter—for cheaply he gets our workers' and peasants' blood!"

Kronstadt lived in deep faith that the proletariat of Petrograd would come to its aid. But the workers there were terrorized, and Kronstadt effectively blockaded and isolated, so that in reality no assistance could be expected from anywhere.

The Kronstadt garrison consisted of less than 14,000 man, 10,000 of them being sailors. This garrison had to defend a widespread front, many forts and batteries scattered over the vast area of the Gulf. The repeated attacks of the Bolsheviks, whom the Central Government continuously supplied with fresh troops; the lack of provisions in the besieged city; the long sleepless nights spent on guard in the cold—all were sapping the vitality of Kronstadt. Yet the sailors heroically persevered, confident to the last that their great example of liberation would be followed throughout the country and thus bring them relief and aid.

In its "Appeal to Comrades Workers and Peasants" the Provisional Revolutionary Committee says:

"Comrades Workers, Kronstadt is fighting for you, for the hungry, the cold, the naked. Kronstadt has raised the banner of rebellion and it is confident that tens of millions of workers and peasants will respond to its call. It cannot be that the daybreak which has begun in Kronstadt should not become bright sunshine for the whole of Russia. It cannot be that the Kronstadt explosion should fail to rouse the whole of Russia and first of all, Petrograd."

But no help was coming, and with every successive day Kronstadt was growing more exhausted. The Bolsheviks continued massing fresh troops against the besieged fortress and weakening it by constant attacks. Moreover, every advantage was on the side of the Communists, including numbers, supplies, and position. Kronstadt had not been built to sustain an assault from the rear. The rumor spread by the Bolsheviks that the sailors meant to bombard Petrograd was false on the face of it. The famous fortress had been planned with the sole view of serving as a defense of Petrograd against foreign enemies approaching from the sea. Moreover, in case the city should fall into the hands of an external enemy, the coast batteries and forts of Krasnaia Gorka had been calculated for a fight against Kronstadt. Foreseeing such a possibility, the builders had purposely failed to strengthen the rear of Kronstadt.

Almost nightly the Bolsheviks continued their attacks. All through March 10 Communist artillery fired incessantly from the southern and northern coasts. On the night of the 12-13 the Communists attacked from the south, again resorting to the white shrouds and sacrificing many hundreds of the *kursanti*. Kronstadt fought back desperately, in spite of many sleepless nights, lack of food and men. It fought most heroically against simultaneous assaults from the north, east and south, while the Kronstadt batteries were capable of defending the fortress only from its western side. The sailors lacked even an ice-cutter to make the approach of the Communist forces impossible.

On March 16 the Bolsheviks made a concentrated attack from three sides at once—from north, south and east. "The plan of attack", later explained Dibenko, formally Bolshevik naval Commissar and later dictator of defeated Kronstadt, "was worked out in minutest detail according to the directions of Commander-in-Chief Tukhachevsky and the field staff of the Southern Corps. At dark we began the attack upon the forts. The white shrouds and the courage of the *kursanti* made it possible for us to advance in columns."

On the morning of March 17 a number of forts had been taken. Through the weakest spot of Kronstadt—the Petrograd Gates—the Bolsheviks broke into the city, and then there began most brutal slaughter. The Communists spared by the sailors now betrayed them, attacking from the rear. Commisar of the Baltic Fleet Kuzmin and Chairman of the Kronstadt Soviet Vassiliev, liberated by the Communists from jail, now participated in hand-to-hand street fighting in fratricidal bloodshed. Until late in the night continued the desperate struggle of the Kronstadt sailors and soldiers against overwhelming odds. The city which for fifteen days had not harmed a single Communist, now ran red with the blood of Kronstadt men, women and even children.

Dibenko, appointed Commissar of Kronstadt, was vested with absolute powers to "clean the mutinous City". An orgy of revenge followed, with the Tcheka claiming numerous victims for its nightly wholesale shooting.

On March 18 the Bolshevik Government and the Communist Party of Russia publicly commemorated the Paris Commune of 1871, drowned in the blood of the French workers by Gallifet and Thiers. At the same time they celebrated the "victory" over Kronstadt.

For several weeks the Petrograd jails were filled with hundreds of Kronstadt prisoners. Every night small groups of them were taken out by order of the Tcheka and disappeared—to be seen among the living no more. Among the last shot was Perepelkin, member of the Provisional Revolutionary Committee of Kronstadt.

The prisons and concentration camps in the frozen district of Archangel and the dungeons a far off Turkestan are slowly doing to death the Kronstadt men who rose against Bolshevik bureaucracy and proclaimed in March, 1921, the slogan of the Revolution of October, 1917: "All Power to the Soviets!"

Author's Afterward: Lessons and Significance of Kronstadt

The Kronstadt movement was spontaneous, unprepared, and peaceful. That it became an armed conflict, ending in a bloody tragedy, was entirely due to the Tartar despotism of the Communist dictatorship.

Though realizing the general character the Bolsheviks, Kronstadt still had faith in the possibility of an amicable solution. It believed the Communist Government amenable to reason; it credited it with some sense of justice and liberty.

The Kronstadt experience proves once more that government, the State—whatever its name or form—is ever the mortal enemy of liberty and self-determination. The state has no soul, no principles. It has but one aim—to secure power and hold it, at any cost. That is the political lesson of Kronstadt.

There is another, a strategic, lesson taught by every rebellion.

The success of the uprising is conditioned in its resoluteness, energy, and aggressiveness. The rebels have on their side the sentiment of the masses. That sentiment quickens with the rising tide of rebellion. It must not be allowed to subside, to pale by a return to the drabness of everyday life.

On the other hand, every uprising has against it the powerful machinery of the State. The Government is able to concentrate in its hands the sources of supply and the means of communication. No time must be given the government to make use of its powers. Rebellion should be vigorous, striking unexpectedly and determinedly. It must not remain localized, for that means stagnation. It must broaden and develop. A rebellion that localizes itself, plays the waiting policy, or puts itself on the defensive, is inevitably doomed to defeat.

In this regard, especially, Kronstadt repeated the fatal strategic errors of the Paris Communards. The latter did not follow the advice of those who favored an immediate attack on Versailles while the Government of Thiers was disorganized. They did not carry the revolution into the country. Neither the Paris workers of 1871 nor the Kronstadt sailors aimed to abolish the Government. The Communards wanted merely certain Republican liberties, and when the Government attempted to disarm them, they drove the Ministers of Thiers from Paris, established their liberties and prepared to defend them — nothing more. Thus also Kronstadt demanded only free elections to the Soviets. Having arrested a few Commissars, the soldiers prepared to defend themselves against attack. Kronstadt refused to act upon the advice of the military experts immediately to take Oranienbaum. The latter was of utmost military value, besides having 50,000 poods of wheat belonging to Kronstadt. A landing in Oranienbaum was feasible, the Bolsheviks would have been taken by surprise and would have had no time to bring up reinforcements. But the sailors did not want to take the offensive, and thus the psychological moment was lost. A few days afterward, when the declarations and acts of the Bolshevik Government convinced Kronstadt that they were involved in a struggle for life, it was too late to make good the error.

The same happened to the Paris Commune. When the logic of the fight forced upon them demonstrated the necessity of abolishing the

Thiers régime not only in their own city but in the whole country, it was too late. In the Paris Commune as in the Kronstadt uprising the tendency toward passive, defensive tactics proved fatal.

Kronstadt fell. The Kronstadt movement for free Soviets was stifled in blood, while at the same time the Bolshevik Government was making compromises with European capitalists, signing the Riga peace, according to which a population of 12 million was turned over to the mercies of Poland, and helping Turkish imperialism to suppress the republics of the Caucasus.

But the "triumph" of the Bolsheviks over Kronstadt held within itself the defeat of Bolshevism. It exposes the true character of the Communist dictatorship. The Communisst proved themselves willing to sacrifice Communism, to make almost any compromise with international capitalism, yet refused the just demands of their own people—demands that voiced the October slogans of the Bolsheviks themselves: Soviets elected by direct and secret ballot, according to the Constitution of the R.S.F.S.R.; and freedom of speech and press for the revolutionary parties.

The Tenth All-Russian Congress of the Communist Party was in session in Moscow at the time of the Kronstadt uprising. At that Congress the whole Bolshevik economic policy was changed as a result of the Kronstadt events and similarly threatening attitude of the people in various other parts of Russia and Siberia. The Bolsheviks preferred to reverse their basic policies, to abolish the *razverstka* (forcible requisition), introduce freedom of trade, give concessions to capitalists and give up communism itself—the communism for which the October Revolution was fought, seas of blood shed, and Russia brought to ruin and despair—but not to permit freely chosen Soviets.

Can anyone still question what the true purpose of the Bolsheviks was? Did they pursue Communist Ideals or Government Power?

Kronstadt is of great historic significance. It sounded the death knell of Bolshevism with its Party dictatorship, mad centralization, Tcheka terrorism and bureaucratic castes. It struck into the very heart of Communist autocracy. At the same time it shocked the intelligent and honest minds of Europe and America into a critical examination of Bolshevik theories and practices. It exploded the Bolshevik myth of the Communist State being the "Workers' and Peasants' Government". It proved that the Communist Party dictatorship and the Russian Revolution are opposites, contradictory and mutually exclusive. It demonstrated that the Bolshevik regime is unmitigated tyranny and reaction, and that the Communist State is itself the most potent and dangerous counter-revolution.

Kronstadt fell. But it fell victorious in its idealism and moral purity, its generosity and higher humanity. Kronstadt was superb. It justly prided itself on not having shed the blood of its enemies, the Communists within its midst. It had no executions. The untutored, unpolished sailors, rough in manner and speech, were too noble to follow the Bolshevik example of vengeance: they would not shoot even the hated Commissars. Kronstadt personified the generous, all forgiving spirit of the Slavic soul and the century-old emancipation movement of Russia.

Kronstadt was the first popular and entirely independent attempt at liberation from the yoke of State Socialism — an attempt made directly by the people, by the workers, soldiers and sailors themselves. It was the first step toward the third Revolution which is inevitable and which, let us hope, may bring to long-suffering Russia lasting freedom and peace.

The Russian Tragedy: (A Review and An Outlook)

Foreword

We live at a time when two civilizations are struggling for their existence. Present society is at death grips with the New Ideal. The Russian Revolution was but the first serious combat of the two forces, whose struggle must continue till the final triumph of the one or of the other.

The Russian Revolution has failed—failed of its ultimate purpose. But that failure is a temporary one. In the point of revolutionizing the thought and feeling of the masses of Russia and of the world, in undermining the fundamental concepts of existing society, and lighting the torch of faith and hope for the Better Day, the Russian Revolution has been of incalculable educational and inspirational value to mankind.

Though the Russian Revolution failed to achieve its true goal, it will forever remain a most magnificent historic event. And yet— tremendous as it is—it is but an incident in the gigantic war of the two worlds.

That war will go on, is going on. In that war capitalism is already facing its doom. Yet more: with capitalism, centralized political government, the state, is also doomed—and that is the most significant lesson of the Russian Revolution as I see it.

This pamphlet was recently published in the Dutch language, whereupon a Holland critic wrote to me: "You have failed to give the full lesson of the Russian Revolution".

I agree with him. It will require a great many volumes to give "the full lesson" of so tremendous an event as the Russian Revolution. My purpose is more modest. It will, require the effort of many minds to clarify to the world the full significance of the Russian Revolution, the potentiality ties of the ideals and ideas involved in it. I merely want to contribute my little share.

I have decided to incorporate the result of my two years' study and observation in Russia in a series of pamphlets under the general caption of the Russian Revolution Series.

The Series will comprise a critical review of the most important phases of the Revolution, together with a constructive analysis of some of the vital lessons to be drawn.

If the present Series will help to make things a little clearer in regard to Russia, if it will aid the workers to see the path of liberation a little straighter, then I shall consider my effort fully repaid.

May, 1922

The Russian Tragedy

It is most surprising how little is known, outside of Russia, about the actual situation and the conditions prevailing in that country. Even intelligent persons, especially among the workers, have the most confused ideas about the character of the Russian Revolution, its development, and its present political, economic and social status. Understanding of Russia and of what has been happening there since 1917 is most inadequate, to say the least. Though the great majority of people side either with or against the Revolution, speak for or against the Bolsheviks, yet almost nowhere is there concrete knowledge and clarity in regard to the vital subjects involved. Generally speaking, the views expressed—friendly or otherwise—are based on very incomplete and unreliable, frequently entirely false, information about the Russian Revolution, its history and the present phase of the Bolshevik regime But not only are the opinions entertained founded, as a rule, on insufficient or wrong data; too often they are deeply colored—properly speaking, distorted—by partisan feeling, personal prejudice, and class interests. On the whole, it is sheer ignorance, in one form or another, which characterizes the attitude of the great majority of people toward Russia and Russian events.

And yet, understanding of the Russian situation is most vital to the future progress and well-being of the world. On the correct estimation of the Russian Revolution, the role played in it by the Bolsheviks and by other political parties and movements, and the causes that have brought about the present situation—in short, on a thorough conception of the whole problem—depends what lessons we shall draw from the great historic events of 1917. Those lessons will, for good or evil, affect the opinions and the activities of great masses of mankind. In other words, coming social changes—and the labor and revolutionary efforts preceding and accompanying them— will be profoundly, essentially influenced by the popular understanding of what has really happened in Russia.

It is generally admitted that the Russian Revolution is the most important historic event since the Great French Revolution. I am even inclined to think that, in point of its potential consequences, the Revolution of 1917 is the most significant fact in the whole known history of mankind. It is the only Revolution which aimed, de facto, at social world revolution; it is the only one which actually abolished the capitalist system on a country-wide scale, and fundamentally altered all social relationships existing till then. An event of such human and historic magnitude must not be judged from the narrow viewpoint of partisanship. No subjective feeling or preconception should be consciously permitted to color one's attitude. Above all, every phase of the Revolution must be carefully studied, without bias or prejudice, and all the facts dispassionately considered, to enable us to form a just and adequate opinion. I believe—I am firmly convinced—that only the whole truth about Russia, irrespective of any considerations whatever, can be of ultimate benefit.

Unfortunately, such has not been the case so far, as a general rule. It was natural, of course, for the Russian Revolution to arouse bitterest antagonism, on the one hand, and most passionate defense, on the other. But partisanship, of whatever camp, is not an objective judge. To speak plainly, the most atrocious lies, as well as ridiculous fairy tales, have been spread about Russia, and are continuing to be spread, even at this late day. Naturally, it is not to be wondered at that the enemies of the Russian Revolution, the enemies of revolution, as such, the reactionaries and their tools, should have flooded the world with most venomous misrepresentation of events transpiring in Russia. About them and their "information" I need not waste any further words: in the eyes of honest, intelligent people they are discredited long ago.

But, sad to state, it is the would-be friends of Russia and of the Russian Revolution who have done the greatest harm to the Revolution, to the Russian people, and to the best interests of the working masses of the world, by their exercise of zeal untempered by truth. Some unconsciously, out of ignorance, but most of them consciously and intentionally have been lying, persistently and cheerfully, in defiance of all facts, in the mistaken notion that they are "helping the Revolution". Reasons of "political expediency", of "Bolshevik diplomacy", of the alleged "necessity of the hour", and frequently motives of less unselfish considerations, have actuated them. The sole legitimate consideration of decent men, of real friends of the Russian Revolution and of man's emancipation, as well as of reliable history—consideration for truth—they have entirely ignored.

There have been honorable exceptions, unfortunately too few: their voice has almost been lost in the wilderness of misrepresentation, falsehood, and overstatement. But most of those who visited Russia simply lied about the conditions in that country—I repeat it deliberately. Some lied because they did not know any better: they had had neither the time nor the opportunity to study the situation, to learn the facts. They made "flying trips", spending ten days or a few weeks in Petrograd and Moscow, unfamiliar with the language, never for a moment coming in direct touch with the real life of the people, hearing and seeing only what was told or shown them by the interested officials accompanying them at every step. In many cases these "students of the Revolution" were veritable innocents abroad, naive to the point of the ludicrous. So unfamiliar were they with the environment that in most cases they had not even the faintest suspicion that their affable "interpreter", so eager to "show and explain everything", was in reality a member of the "trusted men", specially assigned to "guide" important visitors. Many such visitors have since spoken and written voluminously about the Russian Revolution, with little knowledge and less understanding.

Others there were who had the time and the opportunity, and some of them really tried to study the situation seriously, not merely for the purpose of journalistic "copy". During my two years' stay in Russia I had occasion to come in personal contact with almost every foreign visitor, with the Labor missions, and with practically every delegate from Europe, Asia, America and Australia, who gathered in Moscow to attend the, International Communist Congress and the Revolutionary Trade Union Congress held there last year (1921.) Most of them could see and understand what was happening in the country. But it was a rare exception, indeed, that had vision and courage enough to realize that only the whole truth could serve the best interests of the situation.

As a general rule, however, the various visitors to Russia were extremely careless of the truth, systematically so, the moment they began "enlightening" the world. Their assertions frequently bordered on criminal idiocy. Think, for instance, of George Lansbury (publisher of the London "Daily Herald") stating that the ideas of brotherhood, equality, and love preached by Jesus the Nazarene were being realized in Russia—and that at the very time when Lenin was deploring the "necessity of military communism forced upon us by Allied intervention and blockade". Consider the "equality" that divided the population of Russia into 36 categories, according to the ration and wages received. Another Englishman, a noted writer, emphatically claimed that everything would be well in Russia, were it not for outside interference—while whole districts in the East, the South, and in Siberia, some of them larger in area than France, were in armed rebellion against the Bolsheviks and their agrarian policy. Other literati were extolling the "free Soviet system" of Russia, while 18,000 of her sons lay dead at Kronstadt in the struggle to achieve free Soviets.

But why enlarge upon this literary prostitution? The reader will easily recall to mind the legion of Ananiases who have been strenuously denying the very existence of the things that Lenin tried to explain as inevitable. I know that many delegates and others believed that the real Russian situation, if known abroad, might strengthen the hand of the reactionists and interventionists. Such a belief, however, did not necessitate the painting of Russia as a veritable labor Eldorado. But the time when it might have been considered inadvisable to speak fully of the Russian situation is long past. That period has been terminated, relegated into the archives of history, by the introduction of the "new economic policy". Now the time has come when we must learn the full lesson of the Revolution and the causes of its debacle. That we may avoid the mistakes it made (Lenin frankly says they were many), that we be enabled to adopt its best features, we must know the whole truth about Russia.

It is therefore that I consider the present activities of certain labor men as positively criminal and a betrayal of the true interests of the workers of the world. I refer to the men and women, some of them delegates to the Congresses held in Moscow in 1921, that still continue to propagate the "friendly" lies about Russia, delude the masses with roseate pictures of labor conditions in that country, and even seek to induce workers of other lands to migrate in large numbers to Russia. They are strengthening the appalling confusion already existing in the popular mind, deceive the proletariat by false statements of the present and vain promises for the near future. They are perpetuating the dangerous delusion that the Revolution is alive and continuously active in Russia. It is most despicable tactics. Of course, it is easy for an American labor leader, playing to the radical element, to write glowing reports about the condition of the Russian workingmen, while he is being entertained at State expense at the Luxe, the most lucrative hotel in Russia. Indeed, he may insist that "no money is needed", for does he not receive everything his heart desires, free of charge? Or why should the President of an American needleworkers union not state that the Russian workers enjoy full liberty of speech? He is careful not to mention that only Communists and "trusties" were permitted within speaking distance while the distinguished visitor was "investigating" conditions in the factories.

May history be merciful to them.

II

That the reader may form a just estimate of what I shall say further, I think it necessary to sketch, briefly my mental attitude at the time of my arrival in Russia.

It was two years ago. A democratic government, "the freest on earth", had deported me—together with 248 other politicals—from the country I had lived in over thirty years. I had protested emphatically against the moral wrong perpetrated by an alleged democracy in resorting to methods it had so vehemently condemned on the part of the Tsarist autocracy. I branded deportation of politicals as an outrage on the most fundamental rights of man, and I fought it as a matter of principle.

But my heart was glad. Already at the outbreak of the February Revolution I had yearned to go to Russia. But the Mooney case had detained me: I was loath to desert the fight. Then I myself was taken prisoner by the United States, and penalized for my opposition to world slaughter. During two years the forced hospitality of the Federal penitentiary at Atlanta, Ga., prevented my departure. Deportation followed.

My heart was glad, did I say? Weak word to express the passion of joy that filled me at the certainty of visiting Russia. Russia! I was going to the country that had swept Tsardom off the map, I was to behold the land of the Social Revolution! Could there be greater joy to one who in his very childhood had been a rebel against tyranny, whose youth's unformed dreams had envisioned human brotherhood and happiness, whose entire life was devoted to the Social Revolution?!

The journey was an inspiration. Though we were prisoners, treated with military severity, and the *Buford* a leaky old tub repeatedly endangering our lives during the month's odyssey, yet the thought that we were on the way to the land of revolutionary promise kept the whole company of deportees in high spirits, a tremble with expectation of the great Day soon to come. Long, long was the voyage, shameful the conditions we were forced to endure: crowded below deck, living in constant wetness and foul air, fed on the poorest rations. Our patience was nigh exhausted, yet our courage unflagging, and at last we reached our destination.

It was the 19th of January, 1920, when we touched the soil of Soviet Russia. A feeling of solemnity, of awe, almost overwhelmed me. Thus must have felt my pious old forefathers on first entering the Holy of Holies. A strong desire was upon me to kneel down and kiss the ground—the ground consecrated by the life-blood of generations of suffering and martyrdom, consecrated anew by the triumphant revolutionists of my own day. Never before, not even when released from the horrible nightmare of 14 years' prison, had I been stirred so profoundly, longing to embrace humanity, to lay my heart at its feet, to give my life a thousand times, were it but possible, to the service of the Social Revolution. It was the most sublime day of my life.

We were received with open arms. The revolutionary hymn, played by the military Red Band, greeted us enthusiastically as we crossed the Russian frontier. The hurrahs of the red-capped defenders of the Revolution echoed through the woods, rolling into the distance like threats of thunder. With bowed head I stood in the presence of the visible symbols of the Revolution Triumphant. With bowed bead and bowed heart. My spirit was proud, yet meek with the consciousness of actual Social Revolution. What depths, what grandeur lay therein, what incalculable possibilities stretched in its vistas!

I heard the still voice of my soul: "May your past life have contributed, if ever so little, to the realization of the great human ideal, to this, its successful beginning". And I became conscious of the great happiness it offered me: to do, to work, to help with every fiber of my being the complete revolutionary expression of this wonderful people. They had fought and won. They proclaimed the Social Revolution. It meant that oppression has ceased, that submission and slavery, man's twin curses, were abolished. The hope of generations, of ages, has at last been realized; justice has been established upon the earth—at least upon that part of it that was Soviet Russia, and nevermore shall the precious heritage be lost.

But years of war and revolution have exhausted the country. There is suffering and hunger, and much need of stout hearts and willing hands to do and help. My heart sang for joy. Aye, I will give myself fully, completely, to the service of the people; I shall be rejuvenated and grow young again in ever greater effort, in the hardest toil, for the furtherance of the common weal. My very life will I consecrate to the realization of the world's great hope, the Social Revolution.

At the first Russian army outpost a mass meeting was held to welcome us. The large hall crowded with soldiers and sailors, the nun-dressed women on the speaker's platform, their speeches, the whole atmosphere palpitating with Revolution in action—all made a deep impression on me. Urged to say something, I thanked the Russian comrades for their warm welcome of the American deportees, congratulated them on their heroic struggle, and expressed my great joy at being in their midst. And then my whole thought and feeling fused in one sentence. "Dear Comrades", I said, "we came not to teach but to learn; to learn and to help".

Thus I entered Russia. Thus felt my fellow deportees

I remained two years. What I learned, I learned gradually, day by day, in various parts of the country. I had exceptional opportunities for observation and study. I stood close to the leaders of the Communist Party, associated much with the most active men and women, participated in their work, and travelled extensively through the country under conditions most favorable to personal contact with the life of the workers and peasants. At first I could not believe that what I saw was real. I would not believe my eyes, my ears, my judgment. As those trick mirrors that make you appear dreadfully monstrous, so Russia seemed to reflect the Revolution as a frightful perversion. It was an appalling caricature of the new life, the world's hope. I shall not now go into detailed description of my first impressions, my investigations, and the long process that resulted in my final conviction. I fought relentlessly, bitterly, against myself. For two years I fought. It is hardest to convince him who does not want to be convinced. And, I admit, I did not want to be convinced that the Revolution in Russia had become a mirage, a dangerous deception. Long and hard I struggled against this conviction. Yet proofs were accumulating, and each day brought more damning testimony. Against my will, against my hopes, against the holy fire of admiration and enthusiasm for Russia which burned within me, I was convinced—convinced that the Russian Revolution had been done to death.

How and by whom?

III

It has been asserted by some writers that Bolshevik accession to power in Russia was due to a coup, and doubt has been expressed regarding the social nature of the October change.

Nothing could be further from the truth. As a matter of historic fact, the great event known as the October Revolution was in the profoundest sense a social revolution. It was characterized by all the essentials of such a fundamental change. It was accomplished, not by any political party, but by the people themselves, in a manner that radically transformed all the heretofore existing economic, political and social relations. But it did not take place in October. That month witnessed only the formal "legal sanction" of the revolutionary events that had preceded it. For weeks and months prior to it, the actual

Revolution had been going on all over Russia: the city proletariat was taking possession of the shops and factories, while the peasants expropriated the big estates and turned the land to their own use. At the same time workers' committees, peasant committees and Soviets sprang up all over the country, and there began the gradual transfer of power from the provisional government to the Soviets. That took place first in Petrograd, then in Moscow, and quickly spread to the Volga region, the Ural district, and to Siberia. The popular will found expression in the slogan, "All power to the Soviets", and it went sweeping through the length and breadth of the land. The people had risen, the actual Revolution was on. The keynote of the situation was struck by the Congress of the Soviets of the North, proclaiming: "The provisional government of Kerensky must go; the Soviets are the sole power!"

That was on October 10th. Practically all the real power was already with the Soviets. In July the Petrograd uprising against Kerensky was crushed, but in August the influence of the revolutionary workers and of the garrison was strong enough to enable them to prevent the attack planned by Korniloff. The Petrograd Soviet gained strength from day to day. On October 16th it organized its own Revolutionary Military Committee, an act of defiance of and open challenge to the government. The Soviet, through its Revolutionary Military Committee, prepared to defend Petrograd against the coalition government of Kerensky and the possible attack of General Kaledin and his counter-revolutionary Cossacks. On October 22nd the whole proletarian population of Petrograd, solidarically supported by the garrison, demonstrated throughout the city against the government and in favor of "All power to the Soviets".

The All-Russian Congress of Soviets was to open on October 25th. The provisional government, knowing its very existence in imminent peril, resorted to drastic action. On October 23rd the Petrograd Soviet ordered the Kerensky Cabinet to withdraw within 48 hours. Driven to desperation, Kerensky undertook—on October 24th—to suppress the revolutionary press, arrest the most prominent revolutionists of Petrograd, and remove the active Commissars of the Soviet. The government relied on the "faithful" troops and on the young of the military student schools. But it was too late: the attempt to sustain the government failed. During the night of October 24-25 (November 6-7) the Kerensky government was dissolved—peacefully, without bloodshed — and the exclusive supremacy of the Soviets was established. The Communist Party stepped into power. It was the political culmination of the Russian Revolution.

IV

Various factors contributed to the success of the Revolution. To begin with, it met with almost no active opposition: the Russian bourgeoisie was unorganized, weak, and not of a militant disposition. But the main reasons lay in the all-absorbing enthusiasm with which the revolutionary slogans had fired the whole people. "Down with the war!", "Immediate peace!", "The land to the peasant, the factory to the workers!", "All power to the Soviets!" — these were expressive of the passionate soul cry and deepest needs of the great masses. No power could withstand their miraculous effect.

Another very potent factor was the unity of the various revolutionary elements in their opposition to the Kerensky government. Bolsheviks Anarchists, the left faction of the Social Revolutionist party, the numerous politicals freed from prison and Siberian exile, and the hundreds of returned revolutionary emigrants, had all worked during the February-October months toward a common goal.

But if "it was easy to begin" the Revolution, as Lenin had said in one of his speeches, to develop it, to carry it to its logical conclusion was another and more difficult matter. Two conditions were essential to such a consummation: continued unity of all the revolutionary forces, and the application of the country's goodwill initiative and best energies to the important work of the new social construction. It must always be remembered — and remembered well — that revolution does not mean destruction only. It means destruction plus construction, with the greatest emphasis on the plus. Most unfortunately, Bolshevik principles and methods were soon fated to prove a handicap, a drawback upon the creative activities of the masses.

The Bolsheviks are Marxists. Though in the October days they had accepted and proclaimed anarchist watchwords (direct action by the people, expropriation, free Soviets, and so forth), it was not their social philosophy that dictated this attitude. They had felt the popular pulse — the rising waves of the Revolution had carried them far beyond their theories. But they remained Marxists. At heart they had no faith in the people and their creative initiative. As social-democrats they distrusted the peasantry, counting rather upon the support of the small revolutionary minority among the industrial element. They had advocated the Constituent Assembly, and only when they were convinced that they would not have a majority there, and therefore not be able to take State power into their own hands, they suddenly decided upon the dissolution of the Assembly, though the step was a refutation and a denial of fundamental Marxist principles. (Incidentally, it was an Anarchist, Anatoly Zheleznyakov in charge of the palace guard, who took the initiative in the matter). As Marxists, the Bolsheviks insisted on the nationalization of the land: ownership, distribution and control to be in the hands of the State. They were in principle opposed to socialization, and only the pressure of the Left faction of the Social-Revolutionists (the Spiridonova-Kamkov wing) whose influence among the peasantry was traditional, forced the Bolsheviks to "swallow the agrarian program of the Socialist-Revolutionists whole", as Lenin afterwards put it.

From the first days of their accession to political power the Marxist tendencies of the Bolsheviks began to manifest themselves, to the detriment of the Revolution. Social-Democratic distrust of the peasantry influenced their methods and measures. At the All-Russian Conferences the peasants did not receive equal representation with the industrial workers. Not only the village speculator and exploiter, but the agrarian population, as a whole was branded by the Bolsheviks as "petty bosses" and "bourgeois", "unable to keep step with the proletariat on the road to socialism". The Bolshevik government discriminated against the peasant representatives in the Soviets and at the National Conferences, sought to handicap their independent efforts, and systematically narrowed the scope and activities of the Land Commissariat, then by far the most vital factor in the reconstruction of Russia. (The Commissariat was then presided over by a Left Social-Revolutionist). Inevitably this attitude led to much dissatisfaction on the part of the great peasant masses. The Russian *muzhik* is simple and naive, but with the instinct of the primitive man he quickly senses a wrong: no fine dialectics can budge his once settled conviction. The very cornerstone of the Marxian credo, the dictatorship of the proletariat, served as an affront and an injury to the peasantry. They demanded an equal share in the organization and administration of the affairs of the country. Had they not been enslaved, oppressed and ignored long enough? The dictatorship of the proletariat the peasant resented as discrimination against himself. "If dictatorship must be", he argued, "why not of all who labor, of the town worker and of the peasant, together?"

Then came the Brest-Litovsk peace. In its far-reaching results it proved the death blow to the Revolution. Two months previously, in December, 1917, Trotsky had refused, with a fine gesture of noble indignation, the peace offered by Germany on conditions much more favorable to Russia. "We wage no war, we sign no peace!" he had said, and revolutionary Russia applauded him. "No compromise with German imperialism, no concessions", echoed through the length and breadth of the country, and the people stood ready to defend their Revolution to the very death, But now Lenin demanded the ratification of a peace that meant the most mean-spirited betrayal of the greater part of Russia, Finland, Latvia, Lithuania, Ukraine, White Russia, Bessarabia—all were to be turned over to the oppression and exploitation of the German invader and of their own bourgeoisie. It was a monstrous thing—the sacrifice at once of the principles of the Revolution and of its interests as well.

Lenin insisted on ratification, on the ground that the Revolution needed a "breathing spell", that Russia was exhausted, and that peace would enable the "revolutionary oasis" to gather strength for new effort. Radek denounced acceptance of Brest-Litvosk conditions as betrayal of the October Revolution. Trotsky disagreed with Lenin. The revolutionary forces split. The Left Social-Revolutionists, most of the Anarchists and many of the nonpartisan revolutionary elements were bitterly opposed to making peace with imperialism, especially on the terms dictated then by Germany. They declared that such a peace would be fatal to the Revolution; that the principle of "peace without annexations" must not be sacrificed; that the German conditions involved the basest treachery to the workers and peasants of the provinces demanded by the Prussians; that the peace would subject the whole of Russia to economic and political dependence upon German Imperialism, that the invaders would possess themselves of the Ukrainian bread and the Don coal, and drive Russia to industrial ruin.

But Lenin's influence was potent. He prevailed. The Brest-Litvosk treaty was ratified by the 4th Soviet Congress.

It was Trotsky who first asserted in refusing the German peace terms offered in December, 1917, that the workers and peasants, inspired and armed by the Revolution, could by guerilla warfare overcome any army of invasion. The Left Social-Revolutionists now called for peasant uprisings to oppose the Germans, confident that no army could conquer the revolutionary ardor of a people fighting for the fruits of their great Revolution. Workers and peasants, responding, rushed to the aid of Ukraine and White Russia, then valiantly struggling against the German invaders. Trotsky ordered the Russian army to pursue and suppress these partisan units.

The killing of Mirbach followed. It was the protest of the Left Social-Revolutionists Party against, and the defiance of, Prussian imperialism within Russia. The Bolshevik government initiated repressive measures: it now felt itself, as it were, under obligations to Germany. Dzerzhinsky, head of the All-Russian Extraordinary Commission, demanded the delivery of the terrorist. It was a situation unique in revolutionary annals: a revolutionary party in power demanding of another revolutionary party, with which it had till then cooperated, the arrest and punishment of a revolutionist for executing the representative of an imperialist government! The Brest-Litvosk peace had put the Bolsheviks in the anomalous position of a gendarme for the Kaiser. The Left Social-Revolutionists replied to Dzerzhinsky' demand by arresting the latter. This act, and the armed skirmishes which followed it (though insignificant in themselves) were thoroughly exploited by the Bolsheviks politically. They declared that it was an attempt of the Left Social-Revolutionist Party to seize the reins of government. They announced that party outlawed, and their extermination began.

These Bolshevik methods and tactics were not accidental. Soon it became evident that it is the settled policy of the Communist State to crush every form of expression not in accord with the government. After the ratification of the Brest-Litvosk peace the Left Social-Revolutionist Party withdrew its representative in the Soviet of People's Commissars. The Bolsheviks thus remained in exclusive control of the government. Under one pretext and another there followed most arbitrary and cruel suppression of all the other political parties and movements. The Mensheviks and the Right Social-Revolutionists had been "liquidated" long before, together with the Russian bourgeoisie. Now was the turn of the revolutionary elements — the Left Social-Revolutionists the Anarchists, the non-partisan revolutionists.

But the "liquidation" of these involved much more than the suppression of small political groups. These revolutionary elements had strong followings, the Left Social-Revolutionists among the peasantry, the Anarchists mainly among the city proletariat. The new Bolshevik tactics encompassed systematic eradication of every sign of dissatisfaction, stifling all criticism and crushing independent opinion or effort. With this phase the Bolsheviks enter upon the dictatorship over the proletariat, as it is popularly characterized in Russia. The government's attitude to the peasantry is now that of open hostility. More increasingly is violence resorted to. Labor unions are dissolved, frequently by force, when their loyalty to the Communist Party is suspected. The cooperatives are attacked. This great organization, the fraternal bond between city and country, whose economic functions were so vital to the interests of Russia and of the Revolution, is hindered in its important work of production, exchange and distribution of the necessaries of life, is disorganized, and finally completely abolished.

Arrests, night searches, *zassada* (house blockade), executions, are the order of the day. The Extraordinary Commissions (Tcheka), originally organized to fight counter-revolution and speculation, is becoming the terror of every worker and peasant. Its secret agents are everywhere, always unearthing "plots", signifying the *razstrel* (shooting) of hundreds without hearing, trial or appeal. From the intended defense of the Revolution the Tcheka becomes the most dreaded organization, whose injustice and cruelty spread terror over the whole country. All-powerful, owing no one responsibility, the Tchecka is a law unto itself, possesses its own army, assumes police, judicial, administrative and executive powers, and makes its own laws that supersede those of the official State. The prisons and concentration camps are filled with alleged counter-revolutionists and speculators, 95 percent of whom are starved workers, simple peasants, and even children of 10 to 14 years of age. Communism becomes synonymous in the popular mind with Tchekism, the latter the epitome of all that is vile and brutal. The seed of counter-revolutionary feeling is sown broadcast.

The other policies of the "revolutionary government" keep step with these developments. Mechanical centralization, run mad, is paralyzing the industrial and economic activities of the country. Initiative is frowned upon, free effort systematically discouraged. The great masses are deprived of the opportunity to shape the policies of the Revolution, or take part in the administration of the affairs of the country. The government is monopolizing every avenue of life: the Revolution is divorced from the people. A bureaucratic machine is created that is appalling in its parasitism, inefficiency and corruption. In Moscow alone this new class of *sovburs* (Soviet bureaucrats) exceeds, in 1920, the total of office holders throughout the whole of Russia under the Tsar in 1914. The Bolshevik economic policies, effectively aided by this bureaucracy, completely disorganize the already crippled industrial life of the country. Lenin, Zinoviev, and other Communist leaders thunder philippics against the new Soviet bourgeoisie — and issue ever new decrees that strengthen and augment its numbers and influence.

The system of *yedinolitchiye* is introduced: management by one person. Lenin himself is its originator and chief advocate. Henceforth the shop, and factory committees are to be abolished, stripped of all power. Every mill, mine, and factory, the railroads and all the other industries are to be managed by a single head, a "specialist" — and the old Tsarist bourgeoisie is invited to step in. The former bankers, bourse operators, mill owners and factory bosses become the managers, in full control of the industries, with absolute power over the workers. They are vested with authority to hire, employ and discharge the "hands", to give or deprive them of the *payok* (food ration), even to punish them and turn them over to the Tcheka. The workers, who had fought and bled for the Revolution and were willing to suffer, freeze and starve in its defense, resent this unheard-of imposition. They regard it as the worst betrayal. They refuse to be dominated by the very owners and foremen whom they had driven, in the days of the Revolution, out of the factories and who had been so lordly and brutal to them. They have no interest in such a reconstruction. The "new system", heralded by Lenin as the savior of the industries, results in the complete paralysis of the economic life of Russia, drives the workers en masse from the factories, and fills them with bitterness and hatred of everything "socialistic". The principles and tactics of Marxian mechanization of the Revolution are sealing its doom.

The fanatical delusion that a little conspirative group, as it were, could achieve a fundamental social transformation proved the Frankenstein of the Bolsheviks. It led them to incredible depths of infamy and barbarism. The methods of such a theory, its inevitable means, are twofold: decrees and terror. Neither of these did the

Bolsheviks spare. As Bukharin, the foremost ideologue of the militant Communists taught, terrorism is the method by which capitalistic human nature is to be transformed into fit Bolshevik citizenship. Freedom is "a bourgeois prejudice" (Lenin's favorite expression), liberty of speech and of the press unnecessary, harmful. The central government is the depository of all knowledge and wisdom. It will do everything. The sole duty of the citizen is obedience. The will of the State is supreme.

Stripped of fine phrases, intended mostly for Western consumption, this was and is the practical attitude of the Bolshevik government. This government, the real and only actual government of Russia, consists of five persons, members of the inner circle of the Central Committee of the Communist Party of Russia. These "Big Five" are omnipotent. This group, in its true essence conspiratory, has been controlling the fortunes of Russia and of the Revolution since the Brest-Litvosk peace. What has happened in Russia since, has been in strict accord with the Bolshevik interpretation of Marxism. That Marxism, reflected through the Communist inner circle's megalomania of omniscience and omnipotence, has achieved the present debacle of Russia.

In consonance with their theory, the social fundamentals of the October Revolution have been deliberately destroyed. The ultimate object being a powerfully centralized State, with the Communist Party in absolute control, the popular initiative and the revolutionary creative forces of the masses had to be eliminated. The elective system was abolished, first in the army and navy, then in the industries. The Soviets of peasants and worker's were castrated and transformed into obedient Communist committees, with the dreaded sword of the Tcheka ever hanging over them. The labor unions governmentalized, their proper activities suppressed, they were turned into mere transmitters of the orders of the State. Universal military service, coupled with the death penalty for conscientious objectors; enforced labor, with a vast officialdom for the apprehension and punishment of, "deserters"; agrarian and industrial conscription of the peasantry; military Communism in the cities and the system of requisitioning in the country, characterized by Radek as simply grain plundering; the suppression of workers' protests by the use of the military; the crushing of peasant dissatisfaction with an iron hand, even to the extent of whipping the peasants and razing their villages with artillery (in the Ural, Volga and Kuban districts, in Siberia and the

Ukraina)--this characterised the attitude of the Communist State toward the people, this comprised the "constructive social and economic policies" of the Bolsheviks.

Still the Russian peasants and workers, prizing the Revolution for which they had suffered so much, kept bravely fighting on numerous military fronts. They were defending the Revolution, as they thought. They starved, froze, and died by the thousands, in the fond hope that the terrible things the Communists did would soon cease. The Bolshevik horrors were, somehow — the simple Russian thought — the inevitable result of the powerful enemies "from abroad" attacking their beloved country. But when the wars will at last be over — the people naively echoed the official press — the Bolsheviks will surely return to the revolutionary path they entered in October, 1917, the path the wars had forced them temporarily to forsake.

The masses hoped and — endured. And then, at last, the wars were ended. Russia drew an almost audible sigh of relief, relief palpitating with deep hope. It was the crucial moment: the great test had come. The soul of a nation was a-quiver. To be or not to be? And then full realization came. The people stood aghast. Repressions continued, even grew worse. The piratical *razvyorstka*, the punitive expeditions against the peasants, did not abate their murderous work. The Tcheka was unearthing more "conspiracies", executions were taking place as before. Terrorism was rampant. The new Bolshevik bourgeoisie lorded it over the workers and the peasants, official corruption was vast and open, huge food supplies were rotting through Bolshevik inefficiency and centralized State monopoly — and the people were starving.

The Petrograd workers, always in the forefront of revolutionary effort, were the first to voice their dissatisfaction and protest. The Kronstadt sailors, upon investigation of the demands of the Petrograd proletariat, declared themselves solidaric with the workers. In their turn they announced their stand for free Soviets, Soviets free from Communist coercion, Soviets that should in reality represent the revolutionary masses and voice their needs. In the middle provinces of Russia, in the Ukraine, on the Caucasus, in Siberia, everywhere the people made known their wants, voiced their grievances, informed the government of their demands. The Bolshevik State replied with its usual argument: the Kronstadt sailors were decimated, the "bandits" of Ukraine massacred, the "rebels" of the East laid low with machine guns.

This done, Lenin announced at the Tenth Congress of the Communist Party of Russia (March, 1921) that his former policies were all wrong. The *razvyorstka*, the requisition of food, was pure robbery. Military violence against the peasantry a "serious mistake". The workers must receive some consideration. The Soviet bureaucracy is corrupt and criminal, a huge parasite. "The methods we have been using have failed." The people, especially the rural population, are not yet up to the level of Communist principles. Private ownership must be re-introduced; free trade established. Henceforth the best Communist is he who can drive the best bargain. (Lenin's expression).

V

Back to Capitalism!

The present situation in Russia is most anomalous. Economically it is a combination of State and private capitalism. Politically it remains the "dictatorship of the proletariat" or, more correctly, the dictatorship of the inner circle of the Communist Party.

The peasantry has forced the Bolsheviks to make concessions to it. Forcible requisitioning is abolished. Its place has taken the tax in kind, a certain percentage of the peasant produce going to the government. Free trade has been legalized, and the farmer may now exchange or sell his surplus to the government, to the re-established co-operatives or on the open market. The new economic policy opens wide the door of exploitation. It sanctions the right of enrichment and of wealth accumulation. The farmer may now profit by his successful crops, rent more land, and exploit the labor of those peasants who have little land and no horses to work it with. The shortage of cattle and bad harvests in some parts of the country have created a new class of "farm hands" who hire themselves out to the well-to-do peasant. The poor people migrate from those regions which are suffering from famine and swell the ranks of this class. The village capitalist is in the making.

The city worker in Russia today, under the new economic policy, is in exactly the same position as in any other capitalistic country. Free food distribution is abolished except in a few industries operated by the government. The worker is paid wages, and must pay for his necessaries — as in any country. Most of the industries, in so far as they are active, have been let or leased to private persons. The small capitalist now has a free hand. He has a large field for his activities. The farmer's surplus, the product of the industries, of the peasant trades, and of all the enterprises of private ownership, are subject to the ordinary processes of business, can be bought and sold. Competition within the retail trade leads to incorporation and to the accumulation of fortunes in the hands of individuals.

Developing city capitalism and village capitalism cannot long coexist with "dictatorship of the proletariat". The unnatural alliance between the latter and foreign capitalism will in the near future prove another vital factor in the fate of Russia.

The Bolshevik government still strives to uphold the dangerous delusion that the "revolution is progressing", that Russia is "ruled by proletarian soviets", that the Communist Party and its State are identical with the people. It is still speaking in the name of the "proletariat". It is seeking to dupe the people with a new chimera. After awhile — the Bolsheviks now pretend — when Russia shall have become industrially resurrected, through the achievements of our fast growing capitalism, the "proletarian dictatorship" will also have grown strong, and we will return to nationalization. The State will then systematically, curtail and supplant the private industries and thus break the power of the meanwhile developed bourgeoisie.

"After a period of partial denationalization a stronger nationalization begins", says Preobrazhensky, Finance Commissar, in his recent article, "The Perspectives of the New Economic Policy". Then will "Socialism be victorious on the entire front". Radek is less diplomatic. "We certainly do not mean", he assures us in his political analysis of the Russian situation, entitled *Is the Russian Revolution a Bourgeois Revolution?*, "that at the end of a year we shall again confiscate the newly accumulated goods. Our economic policy is based upon a longer period of time. . . . We are consciously preparing ourselves for co-operating with the bourgeoisie; this is undoubtedly dangerous to the existence of the Soviet government, because the latter loses the monopoly on industrial production as against the peasantry. Does not this signify the decisive victory of capitalism? May we not then speak of our revolution as having lost its revolutionary character?!"

To these very timely and significant questions Radek cheerfully replies with a categorical No! It is true, of course, as Marx taught, he admits, that economic relations determine the political ones, and that economic concessions to the bourgeoisie must lead also to political concessions. He remembers that when the powerful landowning class of Russia began making economic concessions to the bourgeoisie those concessions were soon followed by political ones and finally by the capitulation of the landowning class. But he insists that the Bolsheviks will retain their power even under the conditions of the restoration of capitalism. "The bourgeoisie is a historically deteriorating, dying class. . . . That is why the working class (?) of Russia can refuse to make political concessions to the bourgeoisie; since it is justified in hoping that its power will grow on a national and international scale more quickly than will the power of the Russian bourgeoisie".

Meanwhile, though authoritatively assured that his "power is to grow on a national and international scale", the Russian worker is in a bad plight. The new economic policy has made the proletarian "dictator" a common, everyday wage slave, like his brother in countries unblessed with Socialist dictatorship. The curtailment of the government's national monopoly has resulted in the throwing of hundreds of thousands of men and women out of work. Many Soviet institutions have been closed; the remaining ones have discharged from 50 to 75 per cent of their employees. The large influx to the cities of peasants and villagers ruined by the *razvyorstka*, and those fleeing from the famine districts, has produced an unemployment problem of threatening scope. The revival of the industrial life through private capital is a very slow process, due to the general lack of confidence in the Bolshevik State and its promises.

But when the industries will again begin to function more or less systematically, Russia will face a very difficult and complex labor situation. Labor organizations, trade unions, do not exist in Russia, so far as the legitimate activities of such bodies are concerned. The Bolsheviks abolished them long ago. With developing production and capitalism, governmental as well as private, Russia will see the rise of a new proletariat whose interests must naturally come into conflict with those of the employing class. A bitter struggle is imminent. A struggle of a twofold nature: against the private capitalist, and against the State as an employer of labor. It is even probable that the situation may develop still another phase: antagonism of the workers employed in the State-owned industries toward the better-paid workers of private concerns. What will be the attitude of the Bolshevik government? The object of the new economic policy is to encourage, in every way possible, the development of private enterprise and to accelerate the growth of industrialism. Shops, mines, factories and mills have already been leased to capitalists. Labor demands have a tendency to curtail profits; they interfere with the "orderly processes" of business. And as for strikes, they handicap production, paralyze industry. Shall not the interests of Capital and Labor be declared solidaric in Bolshevik Russia?

The industrial and agrarian exploitation of Russia, under the new economic policy, must inevitably lead to the growth of a powerful labor movement. The workers' organizations will unite and solidify the city proletariat with the agrarian poor, in the common demand for better living conditions. From the present temper of the Russian worker, now enriched by his four years' experience of the Bolshevik regime, it may be assumed with considerable degree of probability that the coming labor movement of Russia will develop along syndicalist lines. The sentiment is strong among the Russian workers. The principles and methods of revolutionary syndicalism are not unfamiliar to them. The effective work of the factory and shop committees, the first to initiate the industrial expropriation of the bourgeoisie in 1917, is an inspiring memory still fresh in the minds of the proletariat. Even in the Communist Party itself, among its labor elements, the syndicalist idea is popular. The famous Labor Opposition, led by Shliapnikov and Mme. Kolontay within the Party, is essentially syndicalist.

What attitude will the Bolshevik government take to the labor movement about to develop in Russia, be it wholly or even only partly syndicalist? Till now the State has been the mortal enemy of labor syndicalism within Russia, though encouraging it in other countries. At the Tenth Congress of the Russian Communist Party (March, 1921) Lenin declared merciless warfare against the faintest symptom of syndicalist tendencies, and even the discussion of syndicalist theories was forbidden the Communists, on pain of exclusion from the Party. A number of the Labor Opposition were arrested and imprisoned. It is not to be lightly assumed that the Communist dictatorship could satisfactorily solve the difficult problems arising out of a real labor movement under Bolshevik autocracy. They involve principles of Marxian centralization, the functioning of trade or industrial unions independent of the omnipotent government, and active opposition to private capitalism. But not only the big and small capitalist will the workers of Russia soon have to fight. They will presently come to grips with State capitalism itself.

To correctly understand the spirit and character of the present Bolshevik phase, it is necessary to realize that the so-called "new economic policy" is neither new nor economic, properly considered. It is old political Marxism, the exclusive fountainhead of Bolshevik wisdom. As social-democrats they have remained faithful to their bible. Only a country where capitalism is most highly developed can have a social revolution—that is the acme of Marxian faith. The Bolsheviks are about to apply it to Russia. True, in the October days of the Revolution they repeatedly deviated from the straight and narrow path of Marx. Not because they doubted the prophet. By no means. Rather that Lenin and his group, political opportunists, had been forced by irresistible popular aspiration to steer a truly revolutionary course. But all the time they hung on to the skirts of Marx, and sought every opportunity to direct the Revolution into Marxian channels. As Radek naively reminds us, "already in April, 1918, in a speech by comrade Lenin, the Soviet government attempted to define our next tasks and to point out the way which we now designate as the new economic policy".

Significant admission! In truth, present Bolshevik policies are the continuation of the good orthodox Bolshevik Marxism of 1918. Bolshevik leaders now admit that the Revolution, in its post-October developments, was only political, not social. The mechanical centralization of the Communist State—it must be emphasized—proved fatal to the economic and social life of the country. Violent party dictatorship destroyed the unity of the workers and the peasants, and created a perverted, bureaucratic attitude to revolutionary reconstruction. The complete denial of free speech and criticism, not only to the masses but even to the rank and file of the Communist Party itself, resulted in its undoing, through its own mistakes.

And now? Bolshevik Marxism is continuing in poor Russia. But it is monstrously criminal to prolong this bloody Comedy of Errors. Communist construction is not possible alongside of a sickly capitalism, artificially developed. That capitalism can never be destroyed—as Lenin & Co. pretend to believe—by the regular processes of the Bolshevik State grown economically strong. The "new" policies are therefore a delusion and a snare, fundamentally reactionary. These policies themselves create the necessity for another revolution.

Must tortured humanity ever tread the same vicious circle?

Or will the workers at last learn the great lesson Of the Russian Revolution that every government, whatever its fine name and nice promises is by its inherent nature, as a government, destructive of the very purposes of the social revolution? It is the mission of government to govern, to subject, to strengthen and perpetuate itself. It is high time the workers learn that only their own organized, creative efforts, free from Political and State interference, can make their age-long struggle for emancipation a lasting success.

The Tenth Anniversary of the Russian Revolution

(unpublished manuscript)

It is only a few months now to the tenth anniversary of the October Revolution. Great preparations are being made by the Communist Party and Government of Russia for the celebration of the important event. Numerous committees are at work to make the day the most memorable in the annals of Soviet Russia, and to demonstrate to the country and to the world at large the achievements of the first decade of Bolshevik rule.

There is no doubt that the October Revolution was the most significant social upheaval known in human history. It broke all the molds of established society—not merely political forms, as was the case in previous revolutions, but the very economic foundations that support human slavery and oppression.

The spiritual achievements of the Revolution are tremendous, their ultimate effects immeasurable. It sounded the liberation of a million-headed people that for centuries had been held in bondage. It opened vista of a new civilization of human dignity, brotherhood and freedom. And it lit the torch of hope an inspiration for all the peoples of the world.

A decade is but a short span in the life of a country. It would be near-sighted and unfair to judge the potentialities of new Russia by her actual achievements within the last ten years. But the essential characteristics of Russian life since the Revolution may serve as an indication of the dominant spirit and tendencies of the country.

This is not the place for a detailed review of the first decade of Soviet Russia or even for an approximate estimate of her achievements during that period. It is the fundamental nature and trend of Russian development during the past ten years that are significant, and they are sufficient to clarify the present situation.

Is present-day Russia even in the smallest degree an approach to that purpose? Is it imaginably even on the road toward that end?

Is it enough to state the essential factors of Russian life today to supply the answer.

What are those fundamental factors? What are the essential features that characterize today in Russia and prepare her for tomorrow?

Politically: the most absolute despotism, the exclusive rule of an all-powerful political party that ruthlessly suppresses every symptom of disagreement and non-conformance.

Economically: capitalism, State and private, with all its attending attributes of exploitation, degradation and subjection of the toilers.

Educationally: the apotheosis of the ruling political party, its leaders and the State as omniscient and infallible; the intensification of the spirit of authority and blind obedience; the cultivation of militarist discipline and party chauvinism; the rearing of fanatical subjects whose wills were crippled and minds warped by the elimination of all freedom of speech and the suppression of all but party doctrine and information.

Socially: a condition of terror, with the dominant political party as the sole arbiter of all action, thought and behavior; a regime that cultivates the basest qualities of men by rousing fear, insecurity, hypocrisy and debasement.

These are the vital elements of life under the Bolsheviks. What boots it that Russia has "succeeded" in inducing international capital to exploit her natural resources—and her workers at the same time? Was a great revolution, with all its inevitable bloodshed and suffering, necessary merely to advance Russian development along the lines of American industrialism? Was the Revolution fought to establish modern capitalism in Russia?

It is unspeakably indecent to celebrate these "achievements" of Bolshevik rule in the name of the October Revolution. It is the greatest crime against the spirit of liberty and humanity to rejoice in the betrayal of the Revolution by the Communist Party.

The anniversary of the Revolution can be celebrated only by a revival of the spirit that is now being crushed by the Bolshevik Government. It can be celebrated only be foreswearing tyranny and terror, and by returning to the people the fruits of the Revolution: their liberties and self-determination. In short, by the Bolshevik masters getting off the people's back.

The first step on this road is the absolute abolition of the system of suppression and persecution, and the immediate and unconditional liberation of the political prisoners.

Not a fake liberation of the men and women suffering for opinion's sake, not an "administrative" liberation that will leave the prison doors open for their forced return under some new Tcheka pretext. But an actual liberation guaranteed by the elimination of the least semblance of political persecution.

Thus only can the great October Revolution be fittingly commemorated in spirit and in deed.

Will that be done? Hardly. Certainly not till the Russian people themselves compel the Government to do so. Meanwhile thousands of politicals are rotting in the dungeons of Tcheka or drag out of their miserable existence in the hell-hole of Solovetsky Islands, in the prisons, concentration camps and exile in the most forsaken regions of the Arctic Zone of Northern Russia and Siberia.

It would seem that it were sufficient merely to mention such a terrible state of affairs in an allegedly "revolutionary" country to rouse the indignation of every fair-minded man and woman, and to awaken the conscience of humanity to a liberating deed. But the cries of the victims tortured in Bolshevik prisons and "isolators" remain unheard. Their far-off voices are drowned in the triumphant clamor of the apologists for the terrorism and tyranny of Communist Fascism. Where is the George Kennan to light the torch of fearless truth in Darkest Russia of today?!

The political martyrs in Russia and Siberia need your moral as well as material aid. The "Relief Fund of the International Working Men's Association" is exerting its utmost efforts to help. For that help we depend on you, friends and sympathizers, for without your active support of this worthy cause the imprisoned and exiled politicals in Russia would be doomed to perish from cold and hunger. The allowance that the exiled receive from the Bolshevik government is actually 5 times less than it was under the Romanov regime. In the Turukhen District, for instance (Northwestern Siberia) the politicals used to receive under the Tsar 15 roubles per month for their support. Today they get only 6 roubles and 25 kopecks, while the purchasing value of the rouble is now almost 3 times less than it was in the pre-war days. The Tsar was certainly none too generous to the revolutionists. But today they are practically condemned to death from hunger. Consider then how vital is your help!

The summer is approaching and with it a very critical time in the work of relief. Because during the hot months activists in our movement usually fall off, as a result of which our fund receives but few contributions. We therefore suggest to the various Red Cross and Aid Societies, on whose cooperation we depend (such as those of New York, Chicago, Detroit, etc.), as well as to all our friends and comrades, to bear the situation in mind and to exert themselves to enable us to assist our prisoners and exiles in Russia during the summer. Picnics, entertainments and similar affairs would prove a source of income in behalf of the politicals.

Our Relief fund, which has two sections—one in Paris, the other in Berlin—is intended specially for the benefit of Anarchists and Anarcho-Syndicalists imprisoned or exiled in Russia. We make absolutely no distinction, giving aid to all imprisoned or exiled Anarchists in Russia, to whatever school or group they may belong. In cases where the contributor requests us to divide his donation among other political parties, his instructions are carried out, of course, as shown by the financial accounts in our *Bulletin*. Comrade Emma Goldman, for instance, generally collects at her lectures for the political prisoners of all parties, and funds thus collected and received by us are divided according to the directions of the contributors, local groups, etc.

May those who read these lines take the urgent need of the situation to heart and remember the men and women suffering for their idealism in Russian prisons and exile.

America and the Soviets

(unpublished manuscript)

February, 1931

A great deal is being written now in the Soviet Press about the new American law against convict or forced labor. The United States has recently passed a statute according to which no goods can enter the country that are the product of unfree, forced or convict labor. The new law went into effect in January and there is much discussion in Russia, as well as in the United States, as to what effect the new legislation will have on Russian industrial conditions and on its foreign trade.

The unusual feature of the law is that the burden of proof is laid upon the accused. That is, if Russia attempts to bring its manufactured goods into the United States, it will be up to the Soviets to prove that the goods are not the product of forced or convict labor. Thus, for instance, the United States needs only to charge the Russian importer with bringing in products of forced labor, and then the importer is at once placed under the greatest handicap. Practically it may be equal to debarring the Soviet imports, by burdening the importer with unusual and extraordinary difficulties, for it is almost impossible for Russia to prove that its products are made by "free" labor.

Indeed, how can it be proven that a certain product is the result of free labor? This distinction between so-called "free" labor and "unfree or forced" labor opens the door for endless quibbling and hair-splitting. The interpretation of such a law will depend entirely on the attitude of a given judge or court. One unfriendly to the Soviets would naturally decide against the Russian importer on the mere basis that the Bolshevik Government is an absolute dictatorship, without freedom of action or movement, and that for that very reason labor in Russia cannot be considered free. Such an attitude on the part of the American courts would not be surprising in view of the prevailing American opinion about Russia and also because of certain known facts concerning the Russian workers.

On the other hand, such an interpretation of the law should apply with equal effect to other countries that import goods to the United States. The unprejudiced American citizen may argue that if political dictatorship in Russia involves unfree or forced labor, the same should apply also to importers from other countries that are ruled by dictatorships. In fact, there are today quite a number of lands in Europe whose political form is a dictatorship in this or that form, some of them as absolute as the dictatorship of the Communist Party in Russia. Italy, Poland, Romania—to mention but a few countries— all belong to the same class of political autocracy, however their forms vary.

Furthermore, most European countries import to the United States products of their colonies. In certain of those colonies labor is not only "unfree", but directly and positively forced, in some places even actual slavery, peonage, and other forms of forced toil. It will be seen therefore that such a law involves the greatest complications. Even with the most judicious and liberal application of such a law there must result contradictory decisions, constant friction and a widespread disorganization of the entire world market.

Under such conditions the question would inevitably come up sooner or later as to a final and conclusive decision as to what constitutes "free" and what "unfree, forced" labor. That would indeed be a most interesting problem, but at the same time a veritable Gordian knot. Such a decision could in the last instance be decided only by the Supreme Court of the United States, which is the highest tribunal in that country, charged with interpreting the meaning of laws. On that bench, which consists of 9 persons appointed for life, there often happens to be one or two members, like the late Justice Holmes and now Brandeis, who look at things radically. And so it may happen that a Brandeis may analyze the question of "free" labor and inquire what labor can really be free under existing conditions. For if the proposed new law bars products of unfree, forced labor from other countries, a Brandeis may want to examine if the workers in Europe are so situated that their condition does not force them to labor, as many hours as they are compelled and for such pay as is given them.

It can be seen therefore what ramifications the law under discussion will affect if it becomes a statute and is to be enforced. Just now the bill is before the United States Congress. It is debatable whether that body will take the step that necessarily must very seriously aggravate the great crisis on hand in the United States. For the economic situation there is at present the worst that America has seen in a century, with over seven million out of employment. Russia is doing now 150 million worth of business (in dollars) with the United States, and the amount is growing with each year, and that is a considerable item for a country whose warehouses are bursting with mountains of products that it cannot sell at home. Russia is now one of the best customers for America and the latter country will hardly risk losing that customer by passing a law that would alienate from it Russian business.

The Soviet Government, on the other hand, can also not ignore the danger that threatens it from such a law. To lose its export trade to the United States would be a tremendous blow. Furthermore, other countries, as England, for instance, might follow the example of the United States, and then the barring of the world markets to Russia would bring the worst crisis to her. Russia must look to the matter of forced labor, for that implies work performed by people whose freedom of movement and of choice of employment is restricted by an outer force. It may take the form of prison labor, of toil in concentration camps and lumber clearings, and mass servitude at assigned tasks. In short, it covers all cases where the workers are deprived of liberty, are compelled into a certain environment and deprived of the right or opportunity to alter the conditions under which they labor.

It cannot be denied that to a great extent the workers of Russia are just in that situation. Theoretically, of course, the workers in Russia are their "own bosses", their own employers; they are the "proletarian dictatorship" and they might say, "*L'état c'est moi!*" But unfortunately the reality is quite different. In the establishments that are owned privately in Russia, the workers are, generally speaking, in the same situation as any other workers holding a job with some employer; except that the pay of the Russian worker is much less and his standard of living lower. But the great majority of industries and other factories belong to the State, and there the worker is forbidden by law even to strike. Nor can he leave his job if the conditions do not suit him. Under the 5-year plan migrations of workers have been entirely stopped, and a worker is forbidden to change from one industry to another. He cannot give up his job at will, for in the majority of cases the workers have to sign contracts by which they are pledged to remain at their present jobs until the 5-year plan is completed. Compelled to stay on his present job, the Russian worker is practically a bondsman, without any recourse to striking and without a chance to appeal to his union for redress of grievances, since the union is under the direct control of the Party and the Government.

This situation considered, the proposed American law would indeed be a great blow to Russia. A law debarring products of forced labor could be so interpreted and applied as to exclude from the United States not only the manufactures of Russia but also its products of agriculture. All Marxian theory and Bolshevik arguments notwithstanding, it would be altogether impossible for Soviet Russia to prove to the satisfaction of the world that her labor is "free".

The Anarchist Movement Today

(unpublished manuscript)

1934

The history of human civilization is not a straight, continuously forward-moving line. Its diagram is a zigzag, now advancing, now retreating. Progress is measured by the distance separating man from his primitive conditions of ignorance and barbarism.

At the present time mankind seems to be on the retreat. A wave of reaction is sweeping the countries of Europe; its effects and influence are felt all over the world. There is fascism in Italy, Hitlerism in Germany, despotism in Russia, destructive dictatorship in other countries.

Every progressive and radical party, every revolutionary movement has suffered from the present reaction. In some countries they had been entirely crushed; in others their activities are paralyzed for the time being. It is the essence of all tyrannies and dictatorship, of whatever name or color, to suppress and eradicate everything that stands in the wake of its exclusive domination and triumph. Thus in Russia, for instance, the active anarchist elements (as also the Mensheviks and the Socialist-Revolutionaries) have either been shot or are being kept in prison and exile for indefinite periods. A similar fate has overtaken them in Italy and Germany.

But though anarchism has suffered from the reaction, as have all other liberal and revolutionary movements, it is fundamentally and essentially lost much less than the socialist parties. The reason for it is to be found in certain causes underlying the worldwide reaction. It is generally believe that the war, with its brutalization of man and destruction of higher values, the financial bankruptcy which followed, and the great crisis have brought about the present situation. But these immediate causes are entirely insufficient to explain the incredibly rapid development and success of fascism in Italy and Germany and its spread throughout the civilized world. Other and more potent factors have been at work, resulting in the great reaction.

Those factors are of a psychological rather than a political or economic character. Broadly speaking, there were two of them. One was the Russian Revolution; the other, Marxism.

The Russian Revolution flamed across the world as a beacon of promise and hope to the oppressed and disinherited. It filled the hearts of the masses in every country with inspiration and enthusiasm. The workers of Germany even tried to follow the example of the Russian brothers. But that beacon was soon extinguished. The Bolsheviks, Marxists par excellence by Lenin's interpretation, curbed the popular aspirations of the people and perverted the revolutionary aims and purposes into one of the bloodiest dictatorships the world had ever seen. The despotism of a political party, of a clique, took the place of Tsarist autocracy. The result brought bitter disillusionment to millions of workers in every land, a disillusionment that has proven a powerful aid to the reactionary forces in every land.

Yet that disillusionment would not have necessarily become such an effective lever in the hands of reaction but for another important factor. It was the spirit of authority, of Statism, the worship of government, with which the masses have for years been imbued by Marxism and by the Socialist political parties everywhere. It served to weaken their self-reliance, robbed them of independence in thought and action, and deepened their revolutionary faith and ardor. The Social Democracy of Germany, in particular, has done the greatest harm in this regard. For more than two generations it trained the proletariat in parliamentary inactivity, in systematic compromise, in reliance upon political leaders and in blind authoritarianism. This training lamed the initiative and revolutionary efforts of labor, destroyed the workers' faith in their economic power, and made them dependent on the Marxist Messiah who was to lead them into the promised land of Socialism.

At a certain psychological moment the Messiah came, and the expectant people "heard him gladly". He was not indeed kosher Marxist, but the odor of "socialist" was strong about him and his Nazi party. That sufficed, particularly after the bitter experiences of the German workers with their Socialist governments, which betrayed labor, oppressed and exploited the workers the same as the Junker régimes had done before them.

It is tragic that Socialism, which originated as a liberating movement, has in the course of time become so emasculated of all revolutionary spirit and purpose as to fall a victim to the reactionary Frankenstein it had itself helped to create. If history teaches anything at all, it is this: all progress has been a getting away from authority, a liberation from it—liberation from the authority of the village chief and of the tribal totem: from God, Church and the State. The essence of progress is anti-authoritarian. Man's historic advance has been along the line of more and ever more individual liberty and popular freedom, of greater independence in thought and action, higher culture and improved social well-being. Everything that retarded or hindered that process has served to enslave man and resulted in regress and reaction.

It is because of the above basic truths that the Anarchist movement has suffered much less from the present reaction than have the Socialist parties. The latter now see their organizations annihilated and the millions of their voters become the obedient and submissive followers of the Mussolinis and Hitlers. They did not have enough revolutionary resistance even to put up a fight. More: the very foundations of Socialism are broken, its theories proved false, its methods condemned by experience. Socialism has lost not only its followers but also its ideology. No wonder the Socialist Parties of America, of Sweden and Belgium, the neo-Socialists of France and other countries have now decided to turn from the proletariat to the bourgeoisie for the realization of Socialism!

The Anarchist movement, on the contrary, has sustained only physical, superficial losses. It preserves what is the most vital thing in the life and growth of a world-liberating movement: its ideology, its ideal. Indeed, Anarchism is, essentially, strengthened and verified now by life itself. Parliamentarism has failed utterly. Marxist dogmas have been refuted by experience. Socialist panaceas have been tried and found wanting. The masses will never return to Socialism any more. The experience of Russia and betrayal by Socialist governments in other countries have embittered the workers and made the very name of political Socialism synonymous with treachery and failure.

The present wave of reaction will pass. Experience will teach the people that emancipation from tyranny, oppression and exploitation can be achieved only through Anarchism—in a social organization based on free, solidaric co-operation without any admixture of the vitiating and destructive spirit of authoritarianism. Solidarity without freedom is impossible; it inevitably leads back to slavery, open or masked. The future belongs to Anarchism.

Regarding the condition of the Anarchist movement at the present, the following may be said: Anarchism is not a political party. Its strength cannot be measured by counting heads or ballots. The Anarchist movement is a vital factor of life, based on man's inherent love of liberty and desire for well-being Anarchism finds expression in every form of human endeavor—in the economic and social, as well as in the cultural and artistic phases of existence.

As a movement, Anarchism may be considered in its two-fold aspect: First, as a determining factor in the activities of the masses; and second, as work within the Anarchist organizations themselves, in the groups and federations. As an illustration of mass activity inspired by the ideal and methods of revolutionary Anarchism must serve the labor movement of Spain. Within one year (in February and December, 1933) two revolutionary uprisings have taken place in that country, both of a predominantly Anarcho-Syndicalist character, as expressed by the I.W.M.A. (the International Working Men's Association, known in the European countries as the A.I.T.)

Anarchist groups and federations exist in every country, including Japan, Korea and China. Their work consists in spreading Anarchism by means of the spoken and written word. An approximation of this activity can be gained from the appended list of Anarchist publications in the various countries and languages.

It must be noted, however, that the literature of a great philosophy and social movement like Anarchism is not limited to the newspapers and magazines of Anarchist tendency existing at a given moment. That is accidental, depending on greater or lesser persecution. A true estimate must include, basically, the entire literature on the subject, and its continuous development up to the present.

Anarchist literature does not deal with the superficial, local political or economic conditions of life. It deals with the foundations—social, ethical, cultural, as well as political and economic—that underlie present-day society, and it is idealist in character. It is therefore that Anarchist literature does not go out of date. It keeps its social and practical value, as does philosophy and art, whatever the shallow surface changes in our authoritarian, capitalist civilization.

The finest expression of Anarchist thought and sentiment is to be found in works like William Godwin's *"Enquiry Concerning Political Justice and its Influence on General Virtue and Happiness"* (1793); in the many works of Proudhon, like the keen analysis of 1848 French governmentalism in *"Les Confessions d'un Révolutionnaire"* (1849); in Max Stirner's *"Der Einzige und sein Eigenthum"* (1845); in the numerous writings of Michael Bakunin, some of which are collected in *Oeuvres*, 6 volumes (Paris, 1895-1913); in the *"Idées sur l'Organisation sociale"*, by James Guillaume (1876); in the works of the Italian Anarchist, Errico Malatesta, practical theoretician and active militant from the seventies up to his death in 1932; in *"Les paroles d'un Revolté"*, (composed 1879-1882) by Peter Kropotkin, as well as in the many other works of this Anarchist thinker and scientist; in *"L'Evolution, la Révolution et l'Idéal anarchique"* by Elisée Reclus (1897); in the *"Collected Essays"* of Voltairine de Cleyre, (New York, 1914); in the writings of numerous Spanish Anarchists, such as Ricardo Mella, A. Pellicer Paraire, Tarrida del Marmol, Francisco Ferrer, and others; in the *"Aufruf zum Sozialismus"*, by Gustav Landauer (1911); in the works of Benjamin Tucker, the Individualist Anarchist of America, a man of clear and analytical mind; in those of Josiah Warren, Stephen B. Andrews, Lysander Spooner, Dyer D. Lum, Albert Parsons, C. L. James, Thoreau, William Morris, Edward Carpenter—to name but a few Anglo-Saxon thinkers of Anarchist tendency; in the books and other publications of Ernest Coeurderoy, Carlo Cafiera, Steinlen, Ibsen, Johann Most, Emma Goldman, Rudolf Rocker, Max Nettlau,

Luigi Galleani, and in many other writers, including some memorable pages of Leo Tolstoi.

The Anarchist literature of the world is exceedingly rich. An approximate figure would comprise over 20,000 titles, of which about 3,000 would cover periodicals of longer or shorter duration, issued in 30 or 40 languages in about 40 countries.

"By efficient investigation and careful work on existing materials", writes Dr. Max Nettlau, the erudite Anarchist historian, "a list of this extent could be compiled, with a margin of inaccessible or lost publications, not counting the tens of thousands of smaller items, brochures, leaflets, pictures, etc., and not even referring to the evidence of Anarchist influence in literature, art, the drama".

In the face of these figures, the greater or smaller output of Anarchist literature at a given moment is of little account. The persecution and suppression of Anarchist publications here and there are incidents in a never-ceasing propaganda which has produced efforts of the greatest continuity.

In conclusion I want to say that the Anarchist movement will get bigger and stronger in proportion as the masses will become familiar with Anarchist ideals and ideas and will realize the necessity of putting them into practice. Historic experience and growing disillusionment with all forms of parliamentarism, authoritarianism and dictatorship will gradually make the people understand that emancipation from political oppression, economic slavery and cultural decadence is not possible except under Anarchism — in a society based on individual liberty, equal opportunity and social well-being. The propaganda of Anarchist ideas will help to enlighten the people and enable them the clearer and more intelligently to find the way out of the present stupid and criminal pseudo-civilization. It is therefore that the life, example and propagandistic work of Anarchist individuals and groups are so necessary and vital in furthering the cause of Anarchism.

The Bolshevik Dictatorship At Work

(unpublished manuscript)

It must be left to the future historian to determine whether the Bolshevik repression of the bourgeoisie, with which they started, their rule, was not merely a means towards the ulterior purpose of suppressing all the other non-Bolshevik elements. For the Russian bourgeoisie was not really dangerous to the Revolution. As is well known, it was an insignificant minority, unorganized, without definite solidaric interests and entirely powerless. The revolutionary elements, on the contrary, were a real obstacle to the dictatorship of any political party.

The elimination of the revolutionary elements would be of prime necessity to any dictatorship, because such a dictatorship would meet with the strongest opposition *not* from the bourgeoisie but from the truly revolutionary classes, namely from those that consider dictatorship inimical to the best interests of the Revolution. But the Bolsheviks could not *begin* with the suppression of the revolutionists. It would provoke the disapproval and resistance of the workers and soldiers. It would have to be begun at the bourgeois end and means found gradually to spread the net over the other elements. Distrust and antagonism would have to be wakened, intolerance and persecution stimulated, popular fear roused for the "safety of the

Revolution" in order to secure support for an over-widening campaign of elimination and suppression, for the introduction of the bloody hand of red terror into the life of the Revolution.

As I say, it will be the place of the future historian to determine to what extend such motives have fashioned the policies of the Bolsheviks in 1917 and since. As a matter of fact, the Bolsheviks *did* follow such policies, with the result that their so-called Communist Party became the sole dictator of Russia. Let us now consider, then, what that dictatorship has accomplished in the almost 13 years of its exclusive domination.

First of all, it accomplished the complete mastery of a single political party over a country of over 140 million of people. In the name of the "proletarian dictatorship" the Bolsheviks became the absolute rulers of Russia. But the "proletarian dictatorship" was not and could not be the dictatorship of the proletariat. Millions of people cannot all be dictators. Nor can thousands of party members dictate. By its very nature of dictatorship is limited to a small number of people. The less of them, the stronger and more unified the dictatorship. In actual practice dictatorship *always* means the rule of *one* person, the strong and most unscrupulous man whose will compels the consent of his nominal co-dictators. It cannot be otherwise, and so it was, and is, with the Bolsheviks.

The real dictator in Russia has never been the proletariat, neither the industrial workers nor the agrarian toilers. It is not even the Communist Party. Theoretically the power is wielded by the Central Committee of the Party, but actually it is in the hands of the inner circle of that Committee, called the political bureau or "politbureau". But even the politbureau has never been the real dictator, though its membership is less than a score. In the politbureau there are always differing views on every important question, as there must be where there are many heads, each intriguing for its own political schemes and ambitions. The real dictator is the man whose influence secures the support of the majority of the politbureau. In former days that man was Lenin, and it was he who was the real "proletarian dictatorship", just as Mussolini, for instance, and not the Fascist Party, is dictator in Italy. It was always the views and ideas of Lenin that were carried out, from the very inception of the Bolshevik Party to the last days of Lenin's life; carried out *even* when the entire Party was opposed to his opinion and even when the Central Committee bitterly fought his proposals on their first presentation. It was Lenin who always won, his will that prevailed. It was so in every critical period of Bolshevik history, as I have proved in detail in my recent work "Now and After". It could not help being so, because dictatorship always means domination by the strongest personality, the supremacy of a single will.

As formerly Lenin, so now it is Stalin who single-handedly rules the entire Party, and with it all of Russia. Rules even with a more iron hand that Lenin by simply silencing even the most powerful leaders who happen to disagree with him, as witness the case of Trotsky, Burkharin, Preebrazhensky, Krestinsky and other most powerful co-dictators.

Russia is a country of vast extent, spread over half of Europe and also occupying a goodly part of Asia. It is people by numerous races and nationalities speaking more than fifty different languages and dialects, and having a diversified psychology, varied interests and outlook upon life. We know what the dictatorship of the Tsars did in the pas to that million-headed conglomeration of peoples. Let us now see what the "proletarian" dictatorship has achieved.

Today, over a decade of Bolshevik rule, we can form a fair estimate of its effects and examine the results accomplished. Let us sum them up.

What is Russia today politically? It was the aim of the Revolution to abolish governmental tyranny and oppression and make the people free. The Bolshevik Government is admittedly the worst despotism in Europe, with the sole exception of Fascist rule in Italy. The citizen has no rights which the Government feels bound to respect. The Communist Party is a political monopoly, with all the other parties and movements outlawed. Security of person and domicile is unknown. Freedom of speech and press does not exist. Even within the Party the least difference of opinion is suppressed and punished by imprisonment and exile, as witness the fate of Trotsky and his followers of the Left Opposition. The Right Opposition suffers the same fate, including even the strongest members of the inner circle. One can easily imagine what chances an ordinary mortal has when he dares doubt the omniscience of the Stalin regime. Independent opinion is not tolerated, not to speak of unauthorized motion. The G.P.U — the secret service formerly called the Tcheka — is the super-government with unlimited power over the liberty and lives of the entire people of Russia. Only those who are unquestionably on the side of the dominant Part clique enjoy privileges. They enjoy "full liberty" — the kind of liberty that exists under every despotism: if you have nothing to say you are perfectly free to say it even in the land of Mussolini. As a prominent member of its recent Communist Congress said: "there is room in Russia for all political parties: the Communist Party is in the Government, the others are in prison".

"But even if there is no liberty in Russia", someone may say, "may be the Bolsheviks are benefiting the people economically!" Let us, then, take a look at the economic results of Communist dictatorship.

It was the main purpose of the Revolution to abolish capitalism, free the people from exploitation, break the chains of the material dependence, humiliation and enslavement, and establish Communism and equality.

The Bolshevik dictatorship *began* by instituting a system of the grossest inequality, of unequal compensation and discriminating rewards. At the very beginning of their rule they established 14 different grads of "*payok*" (food rations), discriminating between the sailor and the soldier; between the soldier and the worker; between the worker in one industry and that of another; between the proletarian of the city and the toiler in the fields; between the field toiler and the day laborer; between the latter and the teacher; between the teacher in the industrial field and the instructor in the educational line; between the teacher of lower grades and those who had a university education; and so on, ad infinitum. At one time there in Russia over 25 different "grades" of labor, renumerated differently. Naturally such a condition of "communism" immediately created disaffection and resentment. It was still increased by the fact that a member of the Bolshevik Party, even if not a worker, received a far better ration than the best workingman. And a Bolshevik official received still more, with numerous special privileges that could not fail to arouse the protest of the ordinary proletarian in the factory and shop.

That initial injustice and inequality was *characteristic* of the entire Bolshevik system. Nor were those tactics dictated by the needs of the situation. On the contrary, they were the results merely of political party considerations. Having usurped the reins of government and fearing the opposition of the people, the Bolsheviks sought to strengthen themselves in the government seat by currying favor first of all with the sailors, then with the soldiers and finally with the city workers. But by those means they succeeded only in creating indignation and antagonism in the masses by the crying and obvious injustices. It must never be forgotten that the interest of the masses and their loyalty to a revolution depends *fundamentally* on their feeling that the revolution represents justice and fair play. The masses instinctively see in revolution the enemy of wrong and iniquity; to them the revolution mean the correction of such wrong, their abolition. In this sense revolution is a highly ethical factor and a great inspiration that rouses the people to acts of great self-sacrifice and heroism.

The whole philosophy and tactics of the Bolsheviks ignored this great ethical principle. Initial wrongs paved the way for numerous other and even more terrible injustices. The direct and inevitable result of these policies was to paralyze the economic life of the country. The dictatorship and the red terror by which it was maintained antagonized the people; the new despotism embittered the masses. The repression of every independent effort alienated the best elements from the Revolution and made them feel that it had become the private concern of the political party in power. Facing a new tyranny instead of the longed-for liberty, the workers became discouraged. They felt their revolutionary achievements taken from them and used as a weapon against themselves and their aspirations. The proletarian saw his factory committee subjected to the dictates of the Communist Party and made helpless to protect his interests as a toiler. His labor union became the mouthpiece and transmitter of Bolshevik orders, and he found himself deprived of all voice, not only in the management of industry but even in his own factory where he was kept at work long hours at the poorest pay. The toilers soon realized that the Revolution had been taken out of their hands, that their Soviets had been emasculated of all power, and that their country was being ruled by some people far away in the Kremlin, just as it was in the days of the Tsars. Eliminated from revolutionary and creative activity, living only to obey the new masters, constantly harassed by Bolsheviks and Tchekists, and ever in fear of prison or execution for the least expression of protest, the worker became embittered against the Revolution. He deserted the factory and sought the village where he might be furthest removed from the dreaded rulers and at least secure of his daily bread. Thus broke down the industries of the country.

The peasant saw leather-clad and armed Communists descend upon his quiet village, despoil it of the fruit of his hard labor, and treat him with the brutality and insolence of the old Tsarist officials. He saw his Soviet dominated by some lazy, good-for-nothing village loafer calling himself Bolshevik and holding power from Moscow. He had willingly, even generously, given his wheat and corn to feed the workers and the soldiers, but he saw his provisions lie rotting at the railroad stations and in the warehouses, because the Bolsheviks could not themselves manage things and would let no one else do it. He knew that his brothers in the factory and in the army suffered for lack of food because of Communist inefficiency, bureaucracy, and corruption. He understood why more was always demanded of him. He saw his few possessions, his own family provisions, confiscated by the Tchekists who often took even his last horse without which the peasant could neither work nor live. He saw his neighbor villages, that rebelled against these outrages, leveled to the ground and the peasants whipped and shot, just as in the old days. He turned against the Revolution and in his desperation he determined to plant and sow no more than he needed for himself and family and to hide even that in the forest.

Such were the results of the dictatorship, of Lenin's military communism, and Bolshevik methods. Industry stood still, the bitterness of the workers, and the peasant uprisings began to threaten the existence of the Bolshevik regime. To save the dictatorship Lenin decided to introduce a new economic policy, known as the "NEP".

The purpose of the "NEP" was to revive the economic life of the country. It was to encourage greater production by the peasantry by allowing them to sell their surplus instead of having it forcibly confiscated by the government. It was also to enable exchange of products by legalizing trade and reviving the cooperatives formerly suppressed as counter-revolutionary. But the determination of the Communist Party to hold on to its dictatorship made all these economic reforms ineffectual, because industry cannot develop under a despotic regime. Economic growth, as well as trade and commerce, requires security of person and property, a certain amount of freedom and non-interference in order to function. But dictatorship does not permit that freedom; its "guarantees" cannot inspire confidence. Hence the new economic policy has not produced the results desired, and Russia remains in the throes of poverty, constantly on the brink of economic disaster.

Industrially the dictatorship has emasculated the Revolution of its purpose of placing production in the hands of the proletariat and making the worker independent of economic masters. The dictatorship merely changed masters: the government has become the boss instead of the individual capitalist, though the latter is now also developing as a new clans in Russia. The toiler has remained dependent as before. In fact, more so. His labor organizations have been deprived of all power, and he has lost even the right to strike against his governmental employer. "Since the workers, as a class, wield the dictatorship", the Communists argue, "they cannot strike against themselves". Accordingly the proletarians in Russia pay themselves wages that are not sufficient for bare existence, live crowded in unhygienic quarters, work under most unsanitary conditions, endanger their health and lives because of lack of industrial precaution and safety, and arrest and imprison themselves for an expression of discontent.

Culturally the Bolshevik regime is a training school in Communism and party fanaticism, with no access to ideas differing from the views of the dominant clique. It is the rearing of an entire people in the dogmas of a political church, with no opportunity to broaden and cultivate the mind outside the circle of opinions permitted by the ruling class. No press exists in Russia except the official Communist publications and such others as are approved of by the Bolshevik censor. No public sentiment can find expression there, since the government has a monopoly of speech, press, and assembly.

It is no exaggeration to say that there is less freedom of opinion and opportunity to voice it under the Bolshevik dictatorship than there had been under the Tsars. When Russia was ruled by the Romanovs you could at least secretly issue pamphlets and books, since the government then had no monopoly of the paper supply and printing presses. These were in private hands, and the revolutionists could always find ways to use them for their propaganda.

Today in Russia all the means of publication and distribution are in the exclusive possession of the Government, and no person can express his views to the public unless he first secures Bolshevik permission. Thousands of illegal publications had been issued by revolutionary parties during the autocratic Romanov regime. Under Communist rule such a happening is most exceptional, as witness the indignant amazement of the Bolsheviks when it was discovered that Trotsky had succeeded in publishing the platform of the Opposition element in the Party.

Socially, Bolshevik Russia, ten years after the Revolution, is a country where no man can enjoy political security or economic independence, where the hidden hand of the G.P.U is always at work, terrorizing the people by sudden night searches, arrests for no known cause, secret denunciation for alleged counter-revolution out of personal revenge, imprisonment without hearing or trial, and yearlong exile to the frozen North of Siberia or the arid wastes of Western Asia. A huge prison, where equality means the fear of all alike, and "freedom" signifies unquestioning submission to the powers that be.

Morally, Russia represents the struggle of the finer qualities of man against the degrading and corrupting effects of a system built on coercion and intimidation. The Revolution brought the best instincts of man to the fore: his manhood, his consciousness of human value, his love of liberty and justice. The revolutionary atmosphere inspired and cultivated these tendencies lying dormant in the people, particularly the feeling against oppression, the hunger for freedom, the spirit of mutual helpfulness and cooperation. But the dictatorship has had the effect of counteracting these traits and arousing instead fear and hatred, the spirit of intolerance and persecution. Bolshevik methods have systematically weakened the people's morale, have encouraged servility and hypocrisy, created disillusionment and distrust, and have developed an atmosphere of time-serving now dominant in Russia.

Such is the situation today in that unhappy land, such the effects of the Bolshevik idea that you can make people free by compulsion, the dogma that dictatorship can lead to liberty.

No revolution has yet tried the true way of liberty. None had sufficient faith in it. Force and suppression, persecution, revenge, and terror have characterized all revolutions in the past and have thereby defeated their original aims. The time has come to try new methods, new ways. The social revolution is to achieve the emancipation of man through liberty, but if we have no faith in the latter, revolution becomes a denial and betrayal of itself. Let us then have the courage of freedom: let it replace suppression and terror. Let liberty become our faith and our need, and we shall grow strong therein.

The Paris Commune and Kronstadt

(unpublished manuscript)

March is a historic month: in the struggle of mankind against the power of darkness and oppression it has frequently played a very significant role. But the most important March event of modern times is of comparatively recent date. It took place in Russia just ten years ago in 1921, and is known as the Kronstadt Rebellion.

In many of its characteristics the Kronstadt Rebellion had great similarity with another great historic uprising, namely that of the proletariat of Paris in 1870, which is known as the Paris Commune. The month of March is the anniversary of the Paris Commune, as well the as the Kronstadt Rebellion, and it is fitting that the two great events be celebrated at the same time.

I say "celebrated" advisedly. For though Kronstadt as well as the Paris Commune ended as fearful tragedies, both of them stand out in proletarian history as stirring and momentous struggles for liberty and justice. They are beacon lights, shedding hope and encouragement on the road of emancipation. True, Kronstadt failed of its real purpose just as the Paris Commune had failed, but the very fact of their having been, and having striven and fought with heroic revolutionary idealism is a source of lasting inspiration for the oppressed and disinherited of the world.

On March 18, 1871, the revolutionary proletariat of Paris proclaimed the Commune. There are times when overturning the government can be accomplished without much difficulty. At certain moments the political State crumbles to pieces, like a house of cards, before the first warm breath of the people risen in revolt. Such a time was March, 1871, in France. The people at large were bitter against the government, tired of the war with Germany, and desperate with the suffering caused by tyrannical, oppressive and corrupt rule. Bismarck had dictated his own terms in Versailles and humiliated the French government, and that served to increase the contempt and enmity that the French people felt against the heads of the State.

The moment for a revolution was most propitious. The declaration of the Commune in Paris filled the entire population with the greatest joy. It was felt as a most longed-for deliverance from the hated Versailles tyrants. Even the middle class elements were carried away by the general enthusiasm; they welcomed the most thorough change. The time was ripe, the situation most favorable to revolutionary rebuilding of the country.

Action was necessary and urgent—revolutionary action to put the proletarian aspirations into life, to make the Commune a vital reality, broadening and widening it throughout the entire land.

Alas, he respect for the bourgeois conceptions of law and order, to the sanctity of capitalist property, and faith in the "humanity" of the enemy were soon to turn the great victory of the revolutionary masses into terrible defeat. The first measures of the Commune should have taken was to provide bread for the people. The warehouses were well-stocked, the rich had provided themselves during the war with huge supplies, and the Government and private banks were filled with gold.

But instead of confiscating the accumulated wealth and foodstuffs for the benefit of the starving masses, the Commune made the fatal mistake of wasting precious moments on elections: instead of acting for themselves and organizing the new order of things, the Communard masses confided in their "leaders", entrusted them with taking the initiative and let them pass necessary measures. Known revolutionists were elected by great majorities: Jacobins, Blanquists and Internationalists were represented in the Council of the Commune. But even with the best intentions these revolutionary "leaders" did not know what to do with the Revolution. The masses themselves knew their needs and wants, but the Council of the elected simply proceeded to follow established forms of "governing". They did not even know how to organize the defense of Paris.

Too late the Commune realized that what it most needed was food and not new rules. It began to open communal kitchens to feed the people, but valuable time had been lost which gave Versailles a chance to recover from its great fright and to gather its forces to attack the revolutionary proletariat of Paris. Theirs and Gallifet slaughtered 30,000 workers in the streets of the French capital and drowned the Commune in the blood of its heroic defenders. Dearly did they pay for their mistakes.

The same fearful price had Kronstadt to pay for its faith in governors. Staunch revolutionists and as devoted to their cause as the brave Communards, the men of Kronstadt fell victims to their confidence in the revolutionary integrity of the Bolshevik rulers.

The Kronstadt rebellion of March, 1921, began as a mere expression of sympathy with the striking workers at Petrograd. The sailors and soldiers of Kronstadt were historically the most revolutionary element in Russia. It was they who had been the main strength of the Bolsheviks in their fight against the Provisional Government of Kerensky. They had enabled the Communist Party to upset the Constituent Assembly and to proclaim themselves the new rulers, with Lenin and Trotsky as the dictators in Kremlin. Trotsky had repeatedly declared that without the sailors of Kronstadt the Bolsheviks would have been powerless. He addressed the Kronstadt men as "the pride and glory of the Revolution".

The Kronstadt soldiers and sailors had made common cause with the workers in the October Revolution, fought side-by-side with them, shared their danger hunger, and were indeed true brothers in a common cause. No wonder that when a general strike broke out in Petrograd, on February 24, 1921, the men of Kronstadt stood aghast, as did in fact the entire country. The workers of Petrograd had but a short time before and with their unaided efforts saved Petrograd from the Yudenitch army, and by saving Petrograd they had also saved Moscow and the Revolution. The Bolsheviks had much to thank the Petrograd proletariat for. Its artisans, mechanics and day laborers had served on many fronts; they were the true advance guard of the Revolution and they had sacrificed their blood and all they had in the revolutionary cause.

But conditions in the factories and mills of Petrograd had become unbearable. The work was hard, the rations insufficient, and no clothing was being issued to protect workers against the terrible cold weather. The rule of the Bolsheviks was most draconic and its heavy hand was felt more and more by the workers. But they kept quiet, waiting for the Bolsheviks to make their promises good. A more liberal rule had been solemnly promised them, better rations and more humane treatment, greater liberty and more equal justice — when civil war would be over and the military fronts terminated.

Now the time had come. The soldiers had returned from all fronts and most of them had gone to work on the farms and in the industries. More supplies were available and better means of transportation. The workers of Petrograd, who had suffered most on account of war, revolution and civil strife, were eagerly waiting for the Bolshevik Government to make good its promises.

They waited patiently, a long time, but in vain. Bolsheviks inefficiency and mismanagement continued, their indifference to the country's suffering was unchanged, and the reign of terror even became daily worse.

At last realizing that life could not continue in that situation, that the government was remaining inactive in the matter, the workers at Petrograd decided to come together to consult about their needs and means of alleviating the hunger and distress. They called a meeting for this purpose, but the Government of Petrograd with Zinoviev at its head, promptly suppressed the meeting. Naturally the workers felt outraged by such unjustified and despotic methods. More meetings were called, but these also were forbidden by the Bolsheviks. The workers became outspokenly indignant. They charged that the Bolsheviks were offering most unrevolutionary concessions to the capitalists of Europe and America and that they were making the worst compromises with them, but at the same time the refusing the least rights to the workers of Russia. Feeling against the Communists grew throughout Russia and especially among the proletariat of Petrograd, the most intelligent element of the Russian masses.

Committees were sent to Zinoviev to talk matters over and find some amicable way of coming to understanding. That autocrat, however, refused even to admit the committees to his presence. At last, to compel the government to consider their demands, the workers of Petrograd called the strike. The first to leave work were the men of the Patronny munition factory, and they were followed by those of the Trubotchny and Baltiysky mills. Instead of giving the strikers a hearing, the Petrograd government created a special "Committee of Defense" to suppress the strike movement.

The Committee of Defense immediately declared the strikers as counter-revolutionists, locked them out of the factories and deprived them of their rations, which meant starvation for the men and their families. Strikers' demonstrations were dispersed by the military, arrests multiplied daily, and the entire city was declared under martial law. Deaths at the hand of the Tcheka, from hunger, and cold became an everyday occurrence.

It was these happenings in Petrograd that arouse the sailors and soldiers of Kronstadt. They felt something was radically wrong if the revolutionary proletariat of Petrograd could receive such treatment at the hands of the Bolsheviks. But they refused to take sides in the matter until they have first investigated the situation. If the workers' demands were unjustified or excessive, the sailors declared, Kronstadt would not give them any assistance.

A committee of the sailors quietly came to Petrograd and investigated the claims and demands of the workers. The report of the Committee was submitted to a public meeting of sailors, soldiers and workers of Kronstadt, held on the Yakorny Square on March first. The mas meeting, presided over by the Chairman of the Kronstadt Soviet, the Communist Vassilenko, passed a resolution in favor of the Petrograd strikers and demanding radical reforms of the abuses of the Commissars, as well as the granting of greater liberties by the Bolshevik government.

President Kalinin, who was present at the meeting, and Commissar Kuzmin, head of the Baltic Fleet stationed at Kronstadt, denounced the sailors and Red Army men as counter-revolutionists for demanding free elections for the approaching campaign to select new deputies to the Kronstadt Soviet.

Kronstadt appointed a committee of 30 persons to call on Zinoviev to discuss the situation. That committee was arrested immediately after reaching the city. It was the first blow the Communist Government struck at Kronstadt for daring to express its sympathy with the starving workers of Petrograd.

From that moment on, the situation developed with rapid strides. The Petrograd Soviet, absolutely under the control of Zinoviev, denounced the Kronstadt sailors and workers as counter-revolutionists working in the interest of the Tsar's generals. The same day Lenin and Trotsky issued an ultimatum to Kronstadt to "surrender", and Trotsky had a proclamation spread over Kronstadt by a military flying machine, threatening to "shoot you all like partridges".

Kronstadt asked only justice for the Petrograd strikers and correction of the evils of Commissarship. They were about to elect a new Soviet in their city, and they insisted on the right to act without Communist interference. The sailors and soldiers of Kronstadt issued numerous proclamations, and published a daily Bulletin, affirming their devotion to the Soviet system, their loyalty to the Communist Party, and declaring over and again that they demanded solely their revolutionary rights as proletarians. Repeatedly they called upon the Bolsheviks to settle the dispute in a brotherly, amicable manner, vowing that Revolution and its cause are sacred to them and proclaiming to the whole country, "We want no bloodshed"!

Tragic was the faith of Kronstadt in the revolutionary integrity of their Communist rulers. And while Kronstadt was firm in its intention to persuade the Bolsheviks of its loyalty and devotion to the Communist Party, the latter ordered a secret attack at night upon the unsuspecting city of Kronstadt.

The attack was marshalled by Trotsky, with the expert aid of the military Commissar Tukhatchevsky, a former Tsarist General. Tchekist divisions, wearing white shrouds to blend with the snow-covered Neva River and remaining unseen in the darkness of the night, attacked Kronstadt simultaneously from three sides and finally broke through the gates of the city. Picked Communist troops continued the slaughter on the streets, sparing neither man nor child. Fourteen thousand lives were sacrificed in that internecine strife. For days and nights the nearby Petrograd woods rang with the Tchekist "practice shooting": it was the Kronstadt survivors being executed for the greater glory of the Communist dictators.

The Kronstadt movement was spontaneous, unprepared and peaceful. That it became an armed conflict, ending in a most bloody tragedy, was entirely due to Bolshevik despotism.

The Kronstadt experience, like the Paris Commune, again proves that government—whatever its name or claims—is always the mortal enemy of liberty and justice to the masses. The state has no soul and principles. It has but one aim: to secure power and to hold it, at any cost.

Kronstadt repeated the fatal errors of the Paris Communards. The latter did not follow the advice of the more far-seeing and clearheaded revolutionists who demanded the immediate attack on Versailles while the Government of Thiers was disorganized. They wasted valuable time and they did not carry the revolution into the country, to every nook and corner. Neither the Paris workers of 1871 nor the Kronstadt sailors had set out to abolish the government. The Communards wanted merely certain republican liberties and they believed that a defensive attitude is sufficient protection against the enemy. They failed to assume the aggressive and that proved their undoing

Kronstadt also demanded only some reforms. The sailors refuse to take the aggressive even after it had become clear that the Bolsheviks were preparing to annihilate them. They remained on the defensive and thus lost the psychological moment for victory. The whole of Russia was bitterly antagonistic to the Bolshevik tyranny and passionately in sympathy with Kronstadt. But the latter talked "peace and understanding", while the Communist Government was marshaling artillery against it. In the Paris Commune, as in Kronstadt, the tendency toward passive, defensive tactics and lack of revolutionary clear-sightedness proved fatal.

The Paris Commune and Kronstadt fell. But they fell victorious in their idealism and moral purity, the generosity and higher humanity. The future is theirs.

Just as the Paris Commune, Kronstadt is of utmost historic significance. It sounded the death knell of Bolshevism. It proved to the entire world that the Communist dictatorship and the Russian Revolution are opposites, mutually exclusive. Kronstadt was the first popular attempt at liberation from the tyranny of State Socialism. It was the first step toward the Third Revolution which is inevitable in Russia. May the international proletariat take to heart the lessons of the Paris Commune and of the Kronstadt rebellion to bring to humanity real liberty and well-being and lasting peace to man.

The Awakening Starvelings

(unpublished manuscript)

Ideas are true liberators. Ideas as distinguished from so-called reason. For in our work-a-day world there is much reason and too little thought. It is given only to the seer and poet to conceive liberating ideas—impractical, wild thoughts that ultimately light the way of practical, blind man to better and higher endeavor.

To "practical" minds the regeneration of the world is an empty dream. To transform the cold winter of our age into the warmth of a beautiful summer day, to change our valley of tears and misery into a luxurious garden of joy is a vain fantasy lacking reason and sanity. But a William Morris sees in his mind's eye a world of comradeship and brotherhood rejoicing in the plentitude of earth's bounty, and he challenges "practical reason" to justify the existence of poverty and antagonism in a society over-rich in all the physical and esthetic joys of a full human life.

The incisive genius of a Leonid Andreyev, with a bitter scorn born of intense love, lashes the exasperating helplessness of the great giant of labor, strong enough to support the whole world, yet too weak in spirit and thought to tear to pieces the flimsy network woven about him by the pigmies vampiring on his great body.

How pathetic the helplessness of the giant, mighty in everything save liberating thought!

Ah, indeed, thoughts are not vain fantasies, ideas not an empty dream. Look about you. On every side is being enacted the terrible tragedy of Andreyev's "King Hunger". Labor feeds and clothes the world, while himself, poor Starveling, goes cold and hungry. The Masters of Life tremble in their palaces at the first rumor of their disaffected slaves. Their anxious ear catches the low murmur beneath their feet, the ominous rumbling down in the cellar of life; their faces blanch, and laughter is hushed in the mansions; the temples of Bachanalian joy are deserted, and the bright chandeliers turned low, for fear the starvelings might see the light and find their way to the palaces.

And the Starvelings? They meekly crawl before the trembling masters, the powerful judges by grace of King Hunger, and plead mercy for stealing a five-pound loaf of bread. But the mighty judges know no mercy. The Starvelings are doomed to death. In despair they call to King Hunger, "Help us! Tell us what to do!"

"Revolt" replies Hunger. "Take what is yours".

But how? In the council of the assembled Starvelings, conspiring plans of revolt, there is even greater poverty of thought and liberating ideas than of worldly goods. Ah, the helplessness of the stomach, conscious only of its hunger!

Meek in spirit, poor in thought, the Starvelings again appeal to King Hunger for advice. But he is perfidious, serving with equal impartiality master and slave, ultimately deceiving both. For the despair of Hunger may flame forth in bloody revolt, but it needs the inspiration of the liberating idea to become conscious, triumphant revolution.

Revolts of hunger, inevitable as they often are, are failures in the larger social sense. But revolutions inspired by a liberating idea have always been successful to the degree of their inspiration. And the world progresses. Modern labor is learning the lessons of its past struggles. It is no longer satisfied with the crumbs thrown at it from the masters' heavy-laden tables. It voices its demand, ever more loudly and determinedly, for its full share of life. Over geographical boundaries marches the uprising of the Starvelings. It breaks down national lines, barriers of religion and caste, and sweeps the world with the revolt of the international proletariat. In far China, India and Egypt the coolie is awakening to the new spirit and defying the traditions of centuries. The industrial serfs are challenging their hereditary lords to combat. Throughout the world is to be sensed the coming storm. It is no more the revolt of the Starvelings, blindly following Kind Hunger. It is Revolution, conscious of brotherhood and solidaric unity.

The Idea is the Thing

(unpublished manuscript)

Did you ever ask yourself how it happens that government and capitalism continue to exist in spite of all the evil and trouble they are causing in the world?

If you did, then your answer must have been that it is because the people support those institutions, and that they support them because they believe in them.

That is the crux of the whole matter: present-day society rests on the belief of the people that it is good and useful. It is founded on the idea of authority and private ownership. It is ideas that maintain conditions. Government and capitalism are the forms in which the popular ideas express themselves. Ideas are the foundation; the institutions are the house built upon it.

A new social structure must have a new foundation, new ideas at its base. However you may change the form of an institution, its character and meaning will remain the same as the foundation on which it is built. Look closely at life and you will perceive the truth of this. There are all kinds and forms of government in the world, but their real nature is the same everywhere, as their effects are the same: it always means authority and obedience.

Now, what makes governments exist? The armies and navies? Yes, but only apparently so. What supports the armies and navies? It is the belief of the people, of the masses, that government is necessary; it is the generally accepted idea of the need of government. That is its real and solid foundation. Take the idea or belief away, and no government could last another day.

The same applies to private ownership. The idea that it is right and necessary is the pillar that supports it and gives it security.

Not a single institution exists today but is founded on the popular belief that it is good and beneficial.

Let us take an illustrations; the United States, for instance. Ask yourself why revolutionary propaganda has been of so little effect in that country in spite of fifty years of Socialist, I.W.W. and Anarchist effort. Is the American worker not exploited more intensely than labor in other countries? Is political corruption as rampant in any other land? Is the capitalist class in America not the most arbitrary and despotic in the world? True, the worker in the United States is better situated materially than in Europe, but is he not at the same time treated with the utmost brutality and terrorism the moment he shows the least dissatisfaction? Yet the American worker remains loyal to the government and is the first to defend it against criticism. He is still the most devoted champion of the "grand and noble institutions of the greatest country on earth". Why? Because he believes that they are his institutions, that he, as sovereign and free citizen, is running them and that he could change them if he so wished. It is his faith in the existing order that constitutes its greatest security against revolution. His faith is stupid and unjustified, and some day it will break down and with it American capitalism and despotism. But as long as that faith persists, American plutocracy is safe against revolution.

As men's minds broaden and develop, as they advance to new ideas and lose faith in their former beliefs, institutions begin to change and are ultimately done away with. The people grow to understand that their former views were false, that they were not truth but prejudice and superstition.

In this way many ideas, once held to be true, have come to be regarded as wrong and evil. Thus the ideas of the divine right of kings, of slavery and serfdom. There was a time when the whole world believed those institutions to be right, just, and unchangeable.

In the measure that those superstitions and false beliefs were fought by advanced thinkers, they became discredited and lost their hold upon the people, and finally the institutions that incorporated those ideas were abolished. Highbrows will tell you that they had "outlived their usefulness" and that therefore they "died". But how did they "outlive" their "usefulness?" To whom were they useful, and how did they "die"?

We know already that they were useful only to the master class, and that they were done away with by popular uprisings and revolutions.

Why did not old and effete institutions "disappear" and die off in a peaceful manner?

For two reasons: first, because some people think faster than others. So that it happens that a minority in a given place advance in their views quicker than the rest. The more that minority will become imbued with the new ideas, the more convinced of their truth, and the stronger they will feel themselves, the sooner they will try to realize their ideas; and that is usually before the majority have come to see the new light. So that the minority have to struggle against the majority who still cling to the old views and conditions.

Second, the resistance of those who hold power. It makes no difference whether it is the church, the king, or kaiser, a democratic government or a dictatorship, a republic or an autocracy—those in authority will fight desperately to retain it as long as they can hope for the least chance of success. And the more aid they get from the slower-thinking majority the better the fight they can put up. Hence the fury of revolt and revolution.

The desperation of the masses, their hatred of those responsible for their misery, and the determination of the lords of life to hold on to their privileges and rule combine to produce the violence of popular uprisings and rebellions.

But blind rebellion without definite object and purpose is not revolution. Revolution is rebellion become conscious of its aims. Revolution is social when it strives for a fundamental change. As the foundation of life is economics, the social revolution means the reorganization of the industrial, economic life of the country and consequently also of the entire structure of society.

But we have seen that the social structure rests on the basis of ideas, which implies that changing the structure presupposes changed ideas. In other words, social ideas must change first before a new social structure can be built.

The social revolution, therefore, is not an accident, not a sudden happening. There is nothing sudden about it, for ideas don't change suddenly. They grow slowly, gradually, like the plant or flower. Hence the social revolution is a result, a development, which means that it is evolutionary. It develops to the point when considerable numbers of people have embraced the new ideas and are determined to put them into practice. When they attempt to do so and meet with opposition, then the slow, quiet, and peaceful social evolution becomes quick, militant, and violent. Evolution becomes revolution.

Bear in mind, then, that evolution and revolution are not two separate and different things. Still less are they opposites, as some people wrongly believe. Revolution is merely the boiling point of evolution.

Because revolution is evolution at its boiling point, you cannot "make" a real revolution any more than you can hasten the boiling of a tea kettle. It is the fire underneath that makes it boil: how quickly it will come to the boiling point will depend on how strong the fire is.

The economic and political conditions of a country are the fire under the evolutionary pot. The worse the oppression, the greater the dissatisfaction of the people, the stronger the flame. This explains why the fires of social revolution swept Russia, the most tyrannous and backward country, instead of America where industrial development has almost reached its highest point—and that in spite of all the learned demonstrations of Karl Marx to the contrary.

We see, then, that revolutions, though they cannot be made, can be hastened by certain factors; namely, pressure from above: by more intense political and economic oppression; and by pressure from below: by greater enlightenment and agitation. These spread the ideas; they further evolution and thereby also the coming of revolution.

But pressure from above, though hastening revolution, may also cause its failure, because such revolution is apt to break out before the evolutionary process has been sufficiently advanced. Coming prematurely, as it were, it will fizzle out in mere rebellion; that is, without clear, conscious aim and purpose. At best, rebellion can secure only some temporary alleviation; the real causes of the strife, however, remain intact and continue to operate to the same effect, to cause further dissatisfaction and rebellion.

Summing up what I have said about revolution, we must come to the conclusion that

1) a social revolution is one that entirely changes the foundation of society, its political, economic, and social character;

2) such a change must first take place in the ideas and opinions of the people, in the minds of men;

3) oppression and misery may hasten revolution, but may thereby also turn it into failure, because lack of evolutionary preparation will make real accomplishment impossible;

4) only that revolution can be fundamental, social and successful, which will be the expression of a basic change of ideas and opinions.

From this it obviously follows that the social revolution must be prepared. Prepared in the sense of furthering the evolutionary process, of enlightening the people about the evils of present-day society and convincing them of the desirability and possibility, of the justice and practicability of a social life based on liberty; prepared, moreover, by making the masses realize very clearly just what they need and how to bring it about.

Such preparation is not only an absolutely necessary preliminary step. Therein lies also the safety of the revolution, the only guarantee of its accomplishing its objects.

It has been the fate of most revolutions—as a result of lack of preparation—to be sidetracked from their main purpose, to be misused and led into blind alleys. Russia is the best recent illustration of it. The February Revolution, which sought to do away with the autocracy, was entirely successful. The people knew exactly what they wanted; namely the abolition of Tsardom. All the machinations of politicians, all the oratory and schemes of the Lvovs and Miliukovs—the "liberal" leaders of those days—could not save the Romanov Régime in the face of the intelligent and conscious will of the people. It was this clear understanding of its aims which made the February Revolution a complete success, with, mind you, almost no bloodshed.

Furthermore, neither appeals nor threats by the Provisional Government could avail against the determination of the people to end the war. The armies left the fronts and thus terminated the matter by their own direct action. The will of a people conscious of their objects always conquers.

It was the will of the people again, their resolute aim to get hold of the soil, which secured for the peasant the land he needed. Similarly the city workers, as repeatedly mentioned before, possessed themselves of the factories and of the machinery of production.

So far the Russian Revolution was a complete success. But at the point where the masses lacked the consciousness of definite purpose, defeat began. That is always the moment when politicians and political parties step in to exploit the revolution for their own uses or to experiment their theories upon it. This happened in Russia, as in many previous revolutions. The people fought the good fight—the political parties fought over the spoils to the detriment of the revolution and to the ruin of the people.

This is, then, what took place in Russia. The peasant, having secured the land, did not have the tools and machinery he needed. The worker, having taken possession of the machinery and factories, did not know how to handle them to accomplish his aims. In other words, he did not have the experience necessary to organize production and he could not manage the distribution of the things he was producing.

His own efforts—the worker's, the peasant's, the soldier's—had done away with Tsardom, paralyzed the Government, stopped the war, and abolished private ownership of land and machinery. For that he was prepared by years of revolutionary education and agitation. But for no more than that. And because he was prepared for no more, where his knowledge ceased and definite purpose was lacking, there stepped in the political party and took affairs out of the hands of the masses who had made the revolution. Politics replaced economic reconstruction and thereby sounded the death knell of the social revolution; for people live by bread, by economics, not by politics.

Food and supplies are not created by decree of party or government. Legislative edicts don't till the soil; laws can't turn the wheels of industry. Dissatisfaction, strife, and famine came upon the heels of government coercion and dictatorship. Again, as always, politics and authority proved the swamp in which the revolutionary fires became extinguished.

Let us learn this most vital lesson: thorough understanding by the masses of the true aims of revolution means success. Carrying out their conscious will by their own efforts guarantees the right development of the new life. On the other hand, lack of this understanding and of preparation means certain defeat, either at the hands of reaction or by the experimental theories of would-be political party friends. Let us prepare, then.

The Jobless

(unpublished manucript)

Generally speaking, there is neither any sincere and intelligent plan among the reformers, of whatever hue, to solve this great problem, nor any possibility of a thorough and final solution of unemployment within the legal and industrial boundaries of present-day capitalist society. Unemployment is no sporadic phenomenon of modern life. It is inherent in the character and mode of functioning of our industrial system. The jobless man is always with us, and industrial crises or stagnation, eliminating hundreds of thousands of workers, for a longer or shorter period, from the field of labor, are events of regular and inevitable recurrence.

The causes of unemployment are ridiculously simple, and therefore so little understood. Sociologists, political economists, and reformists have succeeded in so confusing the issue that the real facts of the problem have been all but buried beneath a mass of fictitious issues concerning the tariff, money problems, stringency of the market, and similar aberrations. Yet the fundamental causes underlying all these so-called problems and, above all, the paramount problem of constant unemployment on a comparatively small scale and periodic unemployment for great masses of workers, are only too evident. They are these: the producer, deprived of the full equivalent of his product, cannot buy the latter back. As a result, products accumulate in the hands of the non-producers, till a point is reached when a halt is called to production. Hence closed mills and factories, and men out of work.

In other words: when much food, clothing and shelter has been produced, the producer is thrown out of work and is thus doomed to do without the very things of which we have the greatest abundance. That is to say, the more wealth the worker creates, the poorer he is; the more food on hand, the greater the starvation; the more products are being accumulated, the greater the army of the unemployed.

Surely 'tis no more simple a problem that its existence is a travesty upon all sanity or humanity.

The solution—the only possible one—consists in the producer receiving the full value of his product, or its equivalent. This involves the termination of capitalist production for profit, and the organization of co-operative social production for use.

Such a change in the very fundamentals of capitalist society is inevitable, both for reasons of social necessity as well as because of the growing class consciousness and solidarity of labor. But though inevitable, its accomplishment will require considerable time.

Meanwhile the unemployed by the hundred thousands are tramping the streets of our industrial centers, many of them homeless and hungry. What is being done in this matter by the lords of life, or by the municipal, State and national governments? Why, practically nothing. Even the labor unions, nay, even the Socialist party organs know no better solution to offer than the need of new legislation. And while new laws are being discussed, proposed, voted on and passed, then vetoed or declared unconstitutional, only to be discussed again, amended and passed, and finally found inapplicable or impossible of execution; then labor departments created and commissioners appointed to "investigate thoroughly" the whole situation and catalogue the unemployed by trade, number, nationality, sex, age, and color—while months, aye, years, pass in this graft game of high-paid politicians and reformers—what are the unemployed, hungry and homeless, to do? How are they to exist?

Surely, every hungry man has a right to bread; has a right to demand it, for he is entitled to it by laws more sacred than any man-made statutes—the laws of human need, of self-preservation. And whoever dare refuse a starving man bread, let him take heed. It was Marie Antoinette, if we remember right, who scorned the demand of the Paris mob, when it cried for bread. She probably regretted her *hauteur* when the same "mob" took her head in exchange.

Some Reminiscences of Kropotkin

(unpublished manuscript)

It was about 1890, when the anarchist movement was still in its infancy in America. We were just a handful then, young men and women fired by the enthusiasm of a sublime ideal, and passionately spreading the new faith among the population of the New York Ghetto. We held our gatherings in an obscure hall in Orchard Street, but we regarded our efforts as highly successful. Every week greater numbers attended our meetings, much interest was manifested in the revolutionary teachings, and vital questions were discussed late into the night, with deep conviction and youthful vision. To most of us it seemed that capitalism had almost reached the limits of its fiendish possibilities, and that the Social Revolution was not far off. But there were many difficult questions and knotty problems involved in the growing movement, which we ourselves could not solve satisfactorily. We longed to have our great teacher Kropotkin among us, if only for a short visit, to have him clear up many complex points and to give us the benefit of his intellectual aid and inspiration. And then, what a stimulus his presence would be for the movement!

We decided to reduce our living expenses to the minimum and devote our earnings to defray the expense involved in our invitation to Kropotkin to visit America. Enthusiastically the matter was discussed in group meetings of our most active and devoted comrades; all were unanimous in the great plan. A long letter was sent to our teacher, asking him to come for a lecture tour to America and emphasizing our need of him.

His negative reply gave us a shock: we were so sure of his acceptance, so convinced of the necessity of his coming. But the admiration we felt for him was even increased when we learned the motives for his refusal. He would very much like to come — Kropotkin wrote — and he deeply appreciated the spirit of our invitation. He hoped to visit the United States sometime in the future, and it would give him great joy to be among such good comrades. But just now he could not afford to come at his own expense, and he would not use the money of the movement even for such a purpose.

I pondered over his words. His viewpoint was just, I thought, but it could apply only under ordinary circumstances. His case, however, I considered exceptional, and I deeply regretted his decision not to come. But his motives epitomized to me the man and the grandeur of his nature. I envisioned him as my ideal of revolutionist and Anarchist.

Years later, while I was in the Western Penitentiary of Pennsylvania, the hope of seeing our Grand Old man Kropotkin for a moment illumined the darkness of my cell. Friends had notified me that Peter had come to the States on his way to Canada, where he was to participate in some Congress of scientists. Peter intended to visit me, I was informed, and I counted the days and the hours waiting for the longed-for visit. Alas, the fates were against my meeting my teacher and comrade. Instead of being called to see my dear visitor, I was ordered into the Warden's office. He held in his hand a letter, and I recognized Peter's small and neat handwriting. On the envelope, after my name, Kropotkin had written, "Political Prisoner".

The Warden was in a rage. "We have no political prisoners in our free country!" he roared. And then he tore the envelope into pieces. I became enraged at such desecration. There followed a hot argument on American freedom in the course of which I called the Warden a liar. That was considered *lese majesté* and he demanded an apology. I refused. The result was that instead of meeting Peter I was sentenced to 7 days in the dungeon, which was a cell 2 feet by 4, absolutely dark and 15 feet underground, one small slice of bread as my daily ration.

That was about the year 1895. In the years following Peter Kropotkin had repeatedly visited America, but I never got a chance to see him, because I was mostly in punishment in prison and for ten years I was deprived of visits and not allowed to see anyone. A quarter of a century passed before I could at last take the hand of my old comrade in mine. It was in Russia, in March 1920, that I first met Peter. He lived in Dmitrov, a small town 60 *verats* from Moscow. I was in Petrograd (Leningrad) then, and the railroad conditions were such that traveling from the North to Dmitrov was out of the question. Later on I had a chance to go to Moscow and there I learned that the Government had made special arrangements to enable George Lansbury, the editor of the London *Daily Herald*, and one of his contributors, to visit Kropotkin in Dmitrov. I took advantage of the opportunity, together with our comrades Emma Goldman and A. Schapiro.

Meeting "celebrities" is generally disappointing: rarely does reality tally with the picture of our imagination. But it was not so in the case of Kropotkin; both physically and spiritually he corresponded almost exactly to the mental portrait I had made of him. He looked remarkably like his photographs, with his kindly eyes, sweet smile and generous beard. Every time Kropotkin entered the room it seemed to light up by his presence. The stamp of the idealist was so strikingly upon him, the spirituality of his personality could almost be sensed. But I was shocked at the sight of his emaciation and feebleness.

Kropotkin received the academic *pyock* which was considerably better than the ration issued to the ordinary citizen. But it was far from sufficient to support life and it was a struggle to keep the wolf from the door. The question of fuel and lighting was also a matter of constant worry. The winters were severe and wood very scarce; kerosene difficult to procure, and it was considered a luxury to burn more than one lamp in the house. This lack was particularly felt by Kropotkin; it greatly handicapped his literary labors.

Several times the Kropotkin family had been dispossessed of their home in Moscow, their quarters being requisitioned for government purposes. They then decided to move to Dmitrov. It is only about half a hundred *verats* from the capital, but it might as well be a thousand miles away, so completely was Kropotkin isolated. His friends could rarely visit him; news from the Western world, scientific works, or foreign publications were unattainable. Naturally Kropotkin felt deeply the lack of intellectual companionship and mental relaxation.

I was eager to learn his views on the situation in Russia, but I soon realized that Peter did not feel free to express himself in the presence of the English visitors. The conversation was therefore of a general character. But one of his remarks was very significant and gave me the key to his attitude. "They have shown," he said, referring to the Bolsheviks, "how the Revolution is not to be made." I knew, of course, that as an Anarchist Kropotkin would not accept any Government position, but I wanted to learn why he was not participating in the economic up-building of Russia. Though old and physically weak, his advice and suggestions would be most valuable to the Revolution, and his influence of great advantage and encouragement to the Anarchist movement. Above all, I was interested to hear his positive ideas on the conduct of the Revolution. What I had heard so far from the revolutionary opposition was mostly critical, lacking helpful constructiveness.

The evening passed in desultory talk about the activities on the front, the crime of the Allied blockade in refusing even medicine to the sick, and the spread of disease resulting from lack of food and unhygienic conditions. Kropotkin looked tired, apparently exhausted by the mere presence of visitors. He was old and weak; and I feared he would not live much longer under those conditions. He was evidently undernourished, though he said that the Anarchists of the Ukraine had been trying to make his life easier by supplying him with flour and other products. Makhno, also, when still friendly with the Bolsheviks, had been able to send him provisions. Not to tire Peter too much, we left early.

Some months later I had another opportunity to visit our old comrade. It was summertime and Peter seemed to have revived with the resurrection of Nature. He looked younger, in good health and full of youthful spirit. Without the presence of outsiders, like the former English visitors, he felt more at home with us and we talked freely about Russian conditions, his attitude and the outlook for the future. He was the genial Old Peter again, with a fine sense of humor, keen observation and most generous humanity. At first he chided me solemnly on my stand against the War, but he quickly changed the subject into less dangerous channels. Russia was our main point of discussion. The conditions were terrible, as everyone agreed, and the

Dictatorship the greatest crime of the Bolsheviks. But there was no reason to lose faith, he assured me. The Revolution and the masses were greater than any political Party and its machinations. The latter might triumph temporarily, but the heart of the Russian masses was uncorrupted and they would rally themselves to a clear understanding of the evil of the Dictatorship and of Bolshevik tyranny. Present Russian life, he said, was an artificial condition forced by the governing class. The rule of a small political Party was based on false theories, violent methods, fearful blunders and general inefficiency. They were suppressing the very expression of the people's will and initiative which alone could rebuild the ruined economic life of the country. The stupid attitude of the Allied Powers, the blockade and the attacks on the Revolution by the interventionists, were helping to strengthen the power of the Communist regime. But things will change and the masses will awaken to the realization that no one, no political Party or governmental clique must be permitted in the future to monopolies the Revolution, to control or direct it, for such attempts inevitably result in the death of the Revolution itself.

Various other phases of the Revolution we discussed on that occasion. Kropotkin particularly emphasized the constructive side of revolutions, and especially that the organization of the economic life must be dealt with as the first and greatest necessity of a revolution, as the foundation of its existence and development. This thought he wanted to impress most forcibly upon our own comrades for our guidance in the coming great struggles of the international proletariat.

My visits to our dear Peter were a treat, intellectually and spiritually. I was leaving for the Ukraine for a long tour in behalf of the Petrograd Museum of the Revolution, but I hoped for many more visits to our old, brave teacher of the wonderful brain and heart. It was not to be. He died some months later, on February 8, 1921. I could reach his bedside in time only to say my last farewell to the dead. A great Man, a great Anarchist, had departed.

www.ingramcontent.com/pod-product-compliance
Ingram Content Group UK Ltd.
Pitfield, Milton Keynes, MK11 3LW, UK
UKHW021312180426
11947UKWH00015B/1174